ESSENTIAL GUIDE TO SPANISH READING

Librarians' Selections

AMERICA READS SPANISH

Edited by Lluís Agustí

ESSENTIAL GUIDE TO SPANISH READING: LIBRARIANS' SELECTIONS

ISBN 13: 978-0-9796067-0-0
ISBN 10: 0-9796067-0-5

Edited by Lluís Agustí
Translated by Eduardo de Lamadrid
Revised by Alina San Juan

This is a non commercial edition and is not for sale.
For free copies of this book, contact the Trade Commission of Spain
in Miami at:

TRADE COMMISSION OF SPAIN
2655 LeJeune Rd, Suite 1114
CORAL GABLES, FL 33134
Tel. (305) 446-4387
e-mail: ars@mcx.es
www.americareadsspanish.org

America Reads Spanish is the name of the campaign sponsored by
the Spanish Institute for Foreign Trade and the Spanish Association
of Publishers Guilds, whose purpose is to increase the reading and
use of Spanish through the auspices of thousands of libraries,
schools and booksellers in the United States.

Printed in the United States of America

INTRODUCTIONS & ACKNOWLEDGEMENTS

INTRODUCTIONS

The enhancement of cultural relations with the U.S. should constitute a priority and a developing line of action for Spanish foreign policy with this country. The richness and diversity which characterize contemporary Spanish culture is widely recognized in the U.S., apart from the traditional esteem enjoyed by our linguistic and historical-artistic patrimony, from which derives the prestigious and powerful school of Anglo-American Hispanists.

For said reasons, the diffusion, visibility and knowledge of the Spanish language in the U.S. constitutes a very powerful instrument of influence in diverse spheres of American society, including and prominently so, the political and business sectors, apart from the manifestly social and educational sectors.

As Thomas Jefferson recommended to a nephew in 1787, «Spanish. Bestow great attention on this, and endeavor to acquire an accurate knowledge of it. Our future connections with Spain and Spanish America will render that language a valuable acquisition.»

In the present situation of clear opportunities, to which the growing impact of Americans of Hispanic origin on the national life must be added, it is imperative that we take full advantage of the tools at our disposal to reflect the dynamism of Hispanic letters in a perspicacious manner.

Consequently, an important first step in that direction is attention to the diffusion of books in Spanish, a language whose use grows yearly in this country and which has been the foreign language most in demand in university curriculums for more than 25 years, even before the consolidation of Hispanics as the largest minority in the U.S.

Carlos Westendorp y Cabeza
Ambassador of Spain to the U.S.

INTRODUCTIONS

It is a great pleasure for me to present this *Essential Guide to Spanish Reading*. We have been working on this project for more than a year with the invaluable collaboration of the Spanish Association of Publishers Guilds and the Cervantes Institute of New York.

For several years now, the Spanish Institute for Foreign Trade has been involved in promoting the cultural field by means of its internationalization plan covering industries in the publishing, audiovisual, music and educational service sectors, all of which share a common denominator in the Spanish language. In the United States, this support has crystallized in the promotional plan America Reads Spanish.

This campaign has consolidated itself as an element of continuous communication about all innovations and news relative not only to books in Spanish in the United States, but also to authors, events, opinions and selections by those professionals who have contributed to the publication of this book. It is for us a source of great pride to be able to offer all this information on the web portal www.americareadsspanish.org, flagship of the campaign.

Our objective is to contribute to the promotion of reading in Spanish, which is nothing if not a unifying link for the transmission of Hispanic culture throughout the world.

We are deeply grateful for your participation in this project, and we trust that we can count on you for the improvement and updating of subsequent editions. But above all, we hope that the *Essential Guide to Spanish Reading* will prove to be a useful resource for the compilation and expansion of your book collections in Spanish.

Angel Martín Acebes
Executive Vicepresident / ICEX

INTRODUCTIONS

The Spanish Association of Publishers Guilds, which is also an association of exporters, among other attributes, has had since its inception a patently American focus, conjoined and collaborating with all the professional associations in the region, and stimulating the Spanish presence throughout the American continents.

From that perspective, one of its traditional objectives has been the American market, not only because of its character as the leading market in the world, in which participation is a necessity, but also because of the historical Spanish presence in said market, reinforced in recent years by significant Hispanic-American emigration, which has fomented the use and import of that extraordinary integrative element of the Hispanic-American community which is the Spanish language.

The efforts and labors to strengthen the presence of Hispanic culture and the Spanish language, incumbent on all of us, should prove beneficial to all Hispanic-Americans, particularly in this magnificently creative period for Hispanic culture and literature in Spanish.

The *Essential Guide to Spanish Reading*, created under the sponsorship of the Spanish Institute fof Foreign Trade (ICEX, acronym in Spanish), the Spanish Association of Publishers Guilds (FGEE, acronym in Spanish), and the Trade Commission of Spain, in conjunction with the Ministry of Culture and the Cervantes Institute, is an excellent example of those efforts to increase the presence of Spanish in the modern American market. We trust that the *Guide* presented here, essentially developed by American professionals and whose participation we gratefully acknowledge, will prove to be a useful working tool for all professionals associated with the book trade. At least that was our objective in launching and publishing the work. We are convinced that the objective will be fulfilled.

Jordi Úbeda
President / FGEE

INTRODUCTIONS

This guide to essential works in Spanish, created on the initiative of America Reads Spanish (ARS) is aimed at librarians in the United States and responds to a need which required urgent address: to advise professionals regarding which titles to select, given the voluminous and vast publishing production of Spain and Latin America.

In one sense, this is an eminently practical guide, which aspires to remedy a situation requiring immediate attention, since the number of Spanish speaking readers in the United States is growing at a sustained pace. In another sense, this is also an eclectic guide.

The selection of the 500 titles included herein reflects a strikingly open and democratic process, given that the results are extremely broad and inclusive. The idea which informs it is an undertaking to represent the most varied possible spectrum of works and authors. It is notable that numerous contributors of very diverse backgrounds have collaborated in its preparation. That has allowed the selection to attain an expansive typology, representative of sundry affinities for genres, themes and styles.

To give just one example, the field of narrative includes both highly demanding titles, from the perspective of accessibility and artistic exigencies, and titles of a popular nature, which in conjunction fulfills the important objective of addressing a highly heterogeneous public. It is simply a matter of reaching the greatest number of readers possible. The guide has the rare advantage of offering librarians works which transcend the strictly academic sphere. That same spirit of inclusion encompasses works destined not only for the usual adult readership but also for young readers and children.

Also worth mentioning are the genres covered by this bibliographical selection: in a flexible manner, and with a considerable breadth of outlook, it incorporates representative titles from the multiform genres of imaginative literature, as well as essays, poetry, theater, and—something which is fundamental in a guide addressed to librarians—reference works. Coordinated at the behest of its sponsors at the Cervantes Institute of New York, and accomplished thanks to the generosity and commitment of its Head Librarian, Lluís Agustí, many friends, professors as well as writers, readers at large and representatives of the most diverse professions, have contributed summaries which highlight the plural and participatory nature of the guide.

The differences in the mode of presentation of the books (both in tone and extension) betoken a sign of vitality: they reveal a multiplicity of origins in the recommendations. At the deepest level, this exposes the democratic and representative character of the guide, which could be defined as the result of the sum of individual passions. The collaborators have rescued from their own personal backgrounds reading experiences which they wish to share with the great body of the reading public in the Spanish language in the United States.

Eduardo Lago
Director, Instituto Cervantes New York

INTRODUCTIONS

The Essential Guide to Spanish Reading is another important initiative of the already successful America Reads Spanish (ARS), the campaign to promote reading in Spanish in the United States in collaboration with REFORMA, the National Association to Promote Library and Information Services to Latinos and the Spanish–Speaking.

To explain briefly the contents of this guide, it has been divided into 5 categories: Fiction and Literature; Poetry and Drama; Non-Fiction; Reference and Children / Young Adult Books. Each entry includes a written commentary, a glance into the selector's literary habits and standards as well as personal reading tastes whether for instruction or entertainment. It also indicates if the title is available in English; information of interest to both professionals in charge of developing Latino/Hispanic-interest collections and to publishers.

The Essential Guide to Spanish Reading was truly a nationwide effort to fill a real need for a professional tool for selecting quality works, based not only on the knowledge of book selection criteria but also on the understanding of readers' habits and needs. This was an important undertaking by the ARS with the continued support and contributions by REFORMA members from diverse types of libraries and organizations across the country. This selected guide provides professional recommendations as a basis for the planning and development of Spanish language collections. The vast majority of the selections in this guide are based on recommendations made by librarians who share their knowledge and appreciation for Spanish literature. Journalists, teachers and booksellers were also consulted for their recommendations. In their collective judgment, these are the 500 best books selected by those who drew pleasure or learned from them, so that you can read about them in this guide. Indeed, in my opinion this is an essential guide to quality Spanish-language books available in the United States.

Roxana Benavides
REFORMA President 2006-2007

INTRODUCTIONS

Scope of the *Guide*

In Fall 2006, *America Reads Spanish*[1] launched an on-line survey addressed to librarians in charge of Latin American collections in public, academic and research libraries in the United States of America, so that, in their capacity as experts, they would suggest works germane to the creation of a bibliographic Hispanic database which was initially thought would comprise 500 titles. The works would refer to Spanish letters, language and literatures: fiction, poetry, theater, essays, reference works and children's literature.

Booksellers, writers, professors, editors and journalists also answered this call, and helped to significantly enrich the final results. In March 2007, the compilation of materials was closed with nearly one thousand suggested works. From those recommendations, 500 works, as originally foreseen, were selected for inclusion in the *Guide*.

The Risks of a Plural Endeavor

The open, one might say, choral, nature of this bibliography stems from its own genesis; this is not simply a conventional determination of a canon, rather its value and its richness reside in the fact that the recommended works have been previously read, consulted and used by the professionals who suggested them and who so aver.

The procedure for obtaining the titles in this *Guide* was undoubtedly a risky proposition; precedence was given to free participation over the normative pyramidal process involving literary editors, the distribution of areas of expertise, etc., knowing all the while of the possible disparity in authors, themes, eras and geographic areas which might thus obtain.

---

[1] / America Reads Spanish is the name of the campaign sponsored by the Spanish Institute for Foreign Trade and the Spanish Association of Publishers Guilds, whose purpose is to increase the reading and use of Spanish through the auspices of thousands of libraries, schools and booksellers in the United States.

The final result presented now demonstrates that it was worth assuming that risk. The *Guide* is a rich and plural, distinctive bibliography, and while many of the names listed therein are found in the canons of the most representative works of our literatures, in other instances one will find lesser known or forgotten authors and works, but which nonetheless are of equal import and interest.

Structure of the *Guide*

The bibliography is divided into five major sections: *Fiction, Poetry and Theater, Essays, Reference Works*, and *Children's and Young Adult Literature*. In each section, the works are ordered alphabetically by title. Each reference includes the title in Spanish, its translation into English, a brief note about the work, and the name of the author of the comment and his or her profession and/or place of work; the reference concludes with information about existent published translations of the work into English. It was deemed appropriate not to include information relative to places of publication, publishers, collections, and ISBNs. The *Guide* is further supplemented by general indexes by authors, titles and collaborators.

Usefulness of the *Guide*

The *Guide* aspires to be useful for librarians who wish to endow a basic Hispanic corpus or to complete the one they currently possess with quality works. It may also prove valuable for American booksellers who wish to enrich their offerings for a more demanding readership. Undoubtedly, the *Guide* may also provide practical support in the selection of works for teachers and professors of Spanish and Hispanic literatures. The information about existing translations into English may be helpful to editors and translators; from the bibliography one can appreciate that there are many important work of literature in

Spanish which have not been translated or published in English. Finally, the *Guide* may be used by any reader who seeks advice or suggestions.

Acknowledgments

The first acknowledgment must go to *America Reads Spanish*, creators and sponsors of the idea of the *Guide*, who believed in the usefulness of the project since its inception. Acknowledgments are also due to the following: Eduardo de Lamadrid, for his excellent translations of all the comments and titles, and who also contributed valuable suggestions; Alina San Juan, in charge of, and indispensable to, the final review of the works in the English version; Gaspar Orozco, who brought to the fore his profound knowledge of the entire range of Spanish and Hispanic-American literature and deserves special mention; Nashieli Marcano, who provided an excellent and vast representation of Puerto Rican culture; Richard Heyer, for his support and his very incisive suggestions about Peruvian literature; Adán Griego, for his ability to mobilize librarians and for his vital contributions about Hispanic gay culture; Teresa Mlawer, for her helpful suggestions about children's literature; and Sabrina Abreu and Cristina Fabio, who were instrumental to the development and technical preparation of this *Guide*. The list of acknowledgments concludes with each and every one of the collaborators, whose names appear at the end of the book. Thanks to them all.

Lluís Agustí
Librarian

ACKNOWLEDGEMENTS

We wish to acknowledge the efforts and
dedication of American book distributors
who make books in Spanish available to readers
in the United States.

The following link contains contact
information for those distributors who appear
in the America Reads Spanish webpage:

http://www.americareadsspanish.org/en/distribuidores-inicio.asp

You may contact us at **ars@mcx.es**
to update this information.

CATEGORY INDEX

LITERATURE
FICTION

2666. *(2666)*
Author: Roberto Bolaño
(Not Translated)

The five novels which comprise this monumental work have a common leitmotif based on a historical event: the murders of the women of Juárez. An astonishing display of audacity and narrative power, *2666* blends the structures and essences of the best in European and American narrative, putting itself forward as a new and revolutionary modality of the total novel, which combines traits both of the detective story and the epic poem.
🔹 *Juan Pablo Debesis, Lectorum*

A la deriva y otros cuentos. *(Adrift and Other Tales)*
Author: Horacio Quiroga
(Not Translated)

A collection of short stories by one of Uruguay's finest writers.
🔹 *Scott Van Jacob, University of Notre Dame*

Adán Buenosayres. *(Adán Buenosayres)*
Author: Leopoldo Marechal
(Not Translated)

Without a doubt Marechal's best-known novel, and representative of the transcendent spiritual quality of his work. Based on anecdotes from his childhood and his life, grounded in what might be considered Argentine genre literature, and with an allegorical mission and aim, Adán Buenosayres is truly a literary masterpiece.
🔹 *Lluís Agustí, Instituto Cervantes New York*

Adiós Hemingway. *(Goodbye Hemingway)*
Author: Leonardo Padura
(Not Translated)

Mystery readers and Hemingway fans alike will enjoy the latest case of Padura's postmodern detective Mario Conde. Skeletal remains found in Hemingway's Cuban home require an investigation that leads to revelations about the author's final years.
🔹 *Teresa Chapa, University of North Carolina at Chapel Hill*

Adire y el tiempo roto. *(Adire and Broken Time)*
Author: Manuel Granados
(Not Translated)

The most important Cuban novel written by a black author, its poetic language captivated José Lezama Lima and dazzled Julio Cortázar. One of the great forgotten works of Cuban literature, which again is being discovered by new generations of readers.

🔊 *Fernando Velázquez Medina, Writer and Journalist*

El Aleph. *(El Aleph and Other Stories)*
Author: Jorge Luis Borges
(Translated)

Borges' stories constitute the most influential work in contemporary letters by an author writing in Spanish. And I refer here to the international reading public.

🔊 *Isaías Lerner, CUNY*

La amigdalitis de Tarzán. *(Tarzan's Tonsillitis)*
Author: Alfredo Bryce Echenique
(Translated)

Internationally acclaimed Peruvian writer Alfredo Bryce Echenique portrays in his novel *Tarzan's tonsillitis*, a love story between Juan Manuel Carpio, a composer and singer from Peru, and Fernanda María de la Trinidad del Monte, a Salvadoran married to a Chilean exile. Although their love affair is mostly experienced through their letters, the reader follows their thirty-year relationship through their multiple escapades set in Paris, El Salvador, Chile, California, and London.

🔊 *Libbhy Romero, Brooklyn Public Library*

El amor en los tiempos de cólera. *(Love in the Time of Cholera)*
Author: Gabriel García Márquez
(Translated)

This is my favorite of García Marquez's novels. In his magical style he follows the obsessive love of Florentino for Fermina and after 50 years we all rejoice in the happy reunion and love of the pair.

🔊 *Millie Torrance, Sacramento Public Library*

Amores de segunda mano. *(Second Hand Loves)*
Author: Enrique Serna
(Not Translated)

In this collection of stories, Mexican writer Enrique Serna demonstrates an extraordinary capacity and talent for creating eccentric and perturbed characters, marginalized both socially and sexually. This gallery of the imbalanced is depicted ironically yet affectionately.
 Lluís Agustí, Instituto Cervantes New York

La amortajada. *(The Shrouded Woman)*
Author: María Luisa Bombal
(Translated)

An impressionistic and lyrical account of a woman's life as she lies in her coffin.
Lynn Shirey, Harvard College Library

Antes que anochezca: autobiografía. *(Before Night Falls)*
Author: Reinaldo Arenas
(Translated)

Profoundly human and intensely political award-winning memoir recounts the author's incredible journey from a childhood of poverty in Cuba to his imprisonment for homosexuality, his suppression as a writer and his life in the U.S.
Patricia Cuesta, Los Angeles Public Library

Antología personal. *(Personal Anthology)*
Author: Julio Ramón Ribeyro
(Not Translated)

The intimate relationship between the author and tobacco is analyzed with both humor and fatalism in *For Smokers Only*, the first selection in this compilation from the master of the short story. It also includes essays, plays and diary entries.
Richard Heyer, Instituto Cervantes New York

El árbol de la ciencia. *(The Tree of Knowledge)*
Author: Pío Baroja
(Translated)

The *Tree of Knowledge* belongs to Pío Baroja's trilogy called *The Race* (*La Raza*). This novel about education and reflection on the human condition became an instant classic within the Spanish literary tradition and especially as a psychological work for speculations by the young. It relates the life of Andrés Hurtado, medical student and later village doctor and researcher, a life which is not self-explanatory, which does not have a meaning or absolute reasons to justify it, and in which knowledge and responsibilities are not sources of pleasure but of pain.
🔖 *Lluís Agustí, Instituto Cervantes New York*

Arráncame la vida. *(Mexican Bolero)*
Author: Ángeles Mastretta
(Translated)

If the title sounds like a bolero, it's because the narrative carries the story of a strong woman in post-revolutionary Mexico with such melodic text. And indeed, the English edition was published as *Mexican Bolero* in 1989.
🔖 *Adan Griego, Stanford University Libraries*

El Asco: Thomas Bernhard en El Salvador.
(Disgust: Thomas Bernhard in El Salvador)
Author: Horacio Castellanos Moya
(Not Translated)

Each country should engender a writer who has the capacity of devastating the reader on the page. In the case of El Salvador, Castellanos Moya is that man. In a bitter but brilliant exercise, the protagonist of the book implacably explodes symbols, institutions, characters and everything which constitutes the internal and external life of a country, without distinction to political allegiance or social class. *Disgust* (*El Asco*) is also an exercise in style, an intelligent bomb of acerbic humor. In his fierce but lucid fall, the protagonist will come to the end of himself, understanding that although granted exile, forgetting is denied to him. With novels like *Arms in the Man* (*El Arma en el Hombre*) and *Dance with Serpents* (*Baile con Serpientes*), written in agile and steely prose, Castellanos Moya is without a doubt one of the best and most intense Central American and Hispanic American writers of our times.
🔖 *Gaspar Orozco, Mexican Poet and Diplomat*

Aventuras literarias. *(Literary Adventures)*
Author: Ana C. Jarvis, Raquel Lebredo, and Francisco Mena-Ayllón
(Not Translated)

This book contains short stories written by Latinamerican and Spaniards authors. It also contains classical poetry (Amado Nervo).
🔍 *Guillermina Raffo Magnasco, St Thomas University*

Balún Canán. *(The Nine Guardians: A Novel)*
Author: Rosario Castellanos
(Translated)

A coming-of-age story about a young girl's life on a Chiapas coffee plantation, by the Mexican novelist, poet and diplomat.
🔍 *Lynn Shirey, Harvard College Library*

Barrio de maravillas. *(The Maravillas District)*
Author: Rosa Chacel
(Translated)

In my opinion, this is the greatest novel of 20th century Spanish literature, much more important for the style of its telling and how it provides glimpses of the author's mind than for what it tells. Inward-looking, following the aesthetic theories of Ortega y Gasset, its narrative techniques preceded the French nouveau roman by many years.
🔍 *Juan Carlos Vidal, Instituto Cervantes Chicago*

Las batallas del desierto. *(Battles in the Desert & Other Stories)*
Author: José Emilio Pacheco
(Not Translated)

A minimalist gem from Mexican writer José Emilio Pacheco.
🔍 *Juan Carlos Vidal, Instituto Cervantes Chicago*

Bendíceme, Última. *(Bless Me, Ultima)*
Author: Rudolfo Anaya
(Translated)

Award-winning, uniquely North American coming-of-age novel chronicles the story of an alienated young man in New Mexico who seeks answers to questions about the meaning of life from the magical healer, Última.
🔍 *Patricia Cuesta, Los Angeles Public Library*

El beso de la mujer araña. *(Kiss of the Spider Woman)*
Author: Manuel Puig
(Translated)

Two characters in an Argentine prison during the dictatorship: Valentín Arregui Paz, a political prisoner, and Luis Alberto Molina, a homosexual incarcerated for corrupting minors. Their conversations and Molina's tales based on movies he's seen bring the two men together and enable them to understand one another.
🔎 *Lluís Agustí, Instituto Cervantes New York*

Blanca Sol. *(Blanca Sol)*
Author: Mercedes Cabello de Carbonera
(Not Translated)

A powerful critique of the very restricted role relegated to women in Liman high society at the end of the 19th century. Since Blanca Sol, in spite of her intelligence, has little hope of a fulfilling life of her own, she dedicates herself to manipulating her husband's career and becomes immersed in a frivolous social life.
🔎 *Richard Heyer, Instituto Cervantes New York*

Bomarzo. *(Bomarzo)*
Author: Manuel Mújica Láinez
(Translated)

The refined and cultured Argentine novelist Mújica Láinez wrote one of the most complete and exquisite historical novels in 20th century literature in Spanish. Set in Renaissance Italy, the novel is the fruit of the author's erudition and imaginative gifts. Starting from a painting and Bomarzo's sculpture garden, Mújica Láinez recounts the complex history of hunchback aristocrat, Pier Francesco Orsini.
🔎 *Lluís Agustí, Instituto Cervantes New York*

Caballo de Troya. *(The Trojan Horse)*
Author: J.J. Benítez
(Not Translated)

A novel written about the last weeks in the life of Jesus Christ and about time travel. A series that delves into religious conspiracy theories, especially popular in today's culture.
🔎 *Angela Encinas, San Bernardino Public Library*

Café nostalgia. *(Café Nostalgia)*
Author: Zoé Valdés
(Not Translated)

The author illustrates what it feels to be exiled. Not only from one's country but from one's life.
🔊 *Angela Encinas, San Bernardino Public Library*

Caramelo: puro cuento. *(Caramelo)*
Author: Sandra Cisneros
(Translated)

Inspirational novel by an acclaimed Mexican-American author provides insight into a multigenerational working-class migrant Mexican family as told through the eyes of granddaughter Lala.
🔊 *Patricia Cuesta, Los Angeles Public Library*

La carne de René. *(René's Flesh)*
Author: Virgilio Piñera
(Translated)

«Flesh desires flesh, and the soul seeks its own like,» reads a line by the 15th-century poet Ausiàs March. *René's Flesh* is one of the best-known novels by the renowned Cuban playwright Virgilio Piñera. This fascinating bildungsroman unfolds by using the body as a way to learn via the flesh.
🔊 *Lluís Agustí, Instituto Cervantes New York*

El cartero de Neruda: ardiente paciencia. *(Burning Patience)*
Author: Antonio Skármeta
(Translated)

Chilean writer Antonio Skarmeta depicts in his novel *Burning Patience*, later put into screen to a successful movie, *The Postman,* the friendship between Chile's national poet and Nobel Laureate Pablo Neruda, exiled on Isla Negra, with Mario Jiménez, a young postman whose only duty is to deliver the famous author's mail. Skarmeta sets the story during President Salvador Allende's administration drawing parallels between Mario's private life and romantic involvement with beautiful Beatriz, and the public turbulence and violence that gradually overtakes Chile.
🔊 *Libbhy Romero, Brooklyn Public Library*

La casa de la laguna. *(The House on the Lagoon)*
Author: Rosario Ferré
(Translated)

A family saga set in Puerto Rico and mirroring passions and events through generations of a family. It was nominated for Premio Nacional del Libro in 1995.
🔖 *Millie Torrance, Sacramento Public Library*

La casa de los espíritus. *(The House of the Spirits)*
Author: Isabel Allende
(Translated)

The House of the Spirits is in my opinion Allende's most famous and important book. The multi-generational story of the Trueba family is used to weave an intricate tale of Chilean history, from the early turn of the century through the upheaval and revolution of the 70's.
🔖 *Miriam Rodriguez, Dallas Public Library*

La catedral del mar. *(The Cathedral of the Sea)*
Author: Ildefonso Falcones
(Not Translated)

The most successful new work in Spain in 2006. 🔖 *Julio Rivas, Reader*

Cayo Canas. *(Key Canas)*
Author: Lino Novás Calvo
(Not Translated)

A collection of stories which incorporate the most novel techniques of North American storytelling, as assimilated by this Cuban author born in Galicia, Spain. Displaying great linguistic, stylistic and compositional innovations, this collection placed Novás Calvo at the forefront of Latin American literature.
🔖 *Fernando Velázquez Medina, Writer and Journalist*

Cenizas del querer. *(Ashes of Love)*
Author: Emilia Pereyra
(Not Translated)

Pereyra's second novel transports us to Azua, a small province in southern Dominican Republic, where we discover the complex and false world of Doña Beatriz. In this magical space, where individuals must define themselves, Doña Beatriz encounters social prejudice and endures the moral norms in her rural surroundings.
🔖 *Nashieli Marcano, University of Akron*

Los centroamericanos: antología de cuentos.
(The Central Americans: An Anthology of Stories)
Author: José Mejía, ed.
(Not Translated)

An excellent selection of best short fiction of Central America. A geographic and personal tour consciously effected by some of the best contemporary short stories in some of the more unknown national literatures in Spanish.
 Lluís Agustí, Instituto Cervantes New York

La charca. *(La Charca)*
Author: Manuel Zeno Gandía
(Translated)

This bitter melodrama tells a story about plantation workers' struggle for survival in Puerto Rico in the late 19th century. The beautiful island countryside, contrasted with the starved and diseased human beings who live there, makes this «naturalista» work a classic in Puerto Rican literature.
 Nashieli Marcano, University of Akron

El chico de oro. *(Goldenboy)*
Author: Michael Nava
(Translated)

Nava is one of the great gay Chicano writers. *El chico de oro* was his first novel and introduced us to a gay Chicano detective (Henry Rios) who moved through the California landscape crossing the borders of class and sexuality. Henry Rios appeared in several other mystery novels by Nava. To date, this is the only in Spanish and it deserves a much wider audience.
Adan Griego, Stanford University Libraries

Cien años de soledad. *(One Hundred Years of Solitude)*
Author: Gabriel García Márquez
(Translated)

García Márquez succeeds in captivating readers with the amazingly intricate, epic saga of the mystical town of Macondo as seen through the history of the Buendía family. A must read and a defining classic of twentieth century literature.
Libbhy Romero, Brooklyn Public Library

Cinco horas con Mario. *(Five Hours with Mario)*
Author: Miguel Delibes
(Translated)

It's the mid-60's in Spain, Mario has just died. Menchu, his wife, keeps vigil over the corpse as she recalls in a vibrant and disordered monologue diverse stories and anecdotes of their life in common. From Menchu's reflections, the figure of Mario takes shape —his way of life, his hobbies, his desires, his ideals which stand in stark contrast to those of Spain during the 25 Years of Peace— as well as her own. This impeccable tapestry of memories has been written in such a way that it has been adapted to theater as a monologue.
🔖 *Lluís Agustí, Instituto Cervantes New York*

Cinco maestros: cuentos modernos de Hispanoamérica.
(Five Masters: Modern Hispanic-American Stories)
Author: Alexander Coleman
(Not Translated)

These are short stories from five Latin American authors. The book contains a bilingual vocabulary, which is an enrichment resource for American students.
🔖 *Guillermina Raffo Magnasco, St Thomas University*

Los cipreses creen en Dios. *(The Cypresses Believe in God)*
Author: José María Gironella
(Translated)

When I read it, I was a student in Spain in the year 1978 or 1979. It impressed me so much that every night I dreamt that I was one character or another from the book. Gironella provides the reader not only an understanding, but also a knowledge, an authentic flavor, as it were, of the Spanish Civil War of 1936-1939.
🔖 *Mark Pendleton, Branigan Library Las Cruces NM*

La ciudad de los prodigios. *(The City of Marvels)*
Author: Eduardo Mendoza
(Translated)

Onofre Bouvila, a poor peasant, arrives in Barcelona to work in the World Exhibition of 1888. The story of Bouvila's acquisition of wealth and social ascent, not always in an orthodox manner, runs in parallel to the development of the city of wonder until another key event, the International Exhibition of 1929. One of the best novels written about stirring, turn of the century Barcelona.
🔖 *Lluís Agustí, Instituto Cervantes New York*

La ciudad y los perros. *(The City and the Dogs)*
Author: Mario Vargas Llosa
(Translated)

I was fifteen years old when I read *The City and the Dogs*, Vargas Llosa's first novel. It was my first encounter with great literature and I was dazzled. Silently following the jaguar, the slave and Alberto, I discovered a new and fascinating world, and I decided that I wanted to be a reader.
🖋 *Santiago Cabanas, Cónsul General de España en Miami*

El Club Dumas. *(The Club Dumas)*
Author: Arturo Pérez-Reverte
(Translated)

This is the perfect detective story for a bibliophile. The intrigue involves a rare book detective in search of a banned seventeenth century manuscript of the occult.
🖋 *Teresa Chapa, University of North Carolina at Chapel Hill*

La colmena. *(The Hive)*
Author: Camilo José Cela
(Translated)

Set in the cafés of Madrid and boasting a legion of characters, *La colmena* is a choral novel which masterfully describes the misery of the immediate aftermath of the Civil War. The characters survive hunger, the economic and moral strictures, and above all, the lack of hope, in a sordid and gray atmosphere.
🖋 *Lluís Agustí, Instituto Cervantes New York*

Como agua para chocolate. *(Like Water for Chocolate: A Novel in Monthly Installments, with Recipes, Romances, and Home Remedies)*
Author: Laura Esquivel
(Translated)

USA Today wrote: «This is a charming Mexican love story that will charm the palate and the heart.» It is always checked out and the movie remains very popular.
🖋 *Millie Torrance, Sacramento Public Library*

Condenados de Condado. *(The Condemned of Condado)*
Author: Norberto Fuentes
(Not Translated)

This collection of stories won the Casa de Americas prize in 1968, awarded by a jury chaired by Jorge Edwards. Published in Italy with a prologue by Italo Calvino, the collection evinces a happy amalgam of the styles of Hemingway and Babel. A Cuban short story classic.
Fernando Velázquez Medina, Writer and Journalist

Conspiración Maine. *(The Maine Conspirancy)*
Author: Mario Escobar Golderos
(Not Translated)

Conspiración Maine is a very interesting historical thriller about the sinking of the battleship Maine in the port of Havana in February 1898. It convincingly depicts U.S. aspirations for political dominance, as well as the old Spanish empire in the throes of decadence. Two secret agents, a young female reporter and a professor, will have to discover what's behind the sinking of the ship. A secret organization called the Knights of Columbus stands in their way. A true adventure story full of surprising twists and an exciting ending.
Ángel Santiago Cervantes, Cahesa

Conversación en la catedral. *(Conversation in the Cathedral)*
Author: Mario Vargas Llosa
(Translated)

Political corruption in Peru in the 1950's during a military regime.
Millie Torrance, Sacramento Public Library

El corazón del tártaro. *(The Heart of the Tartar)*
Author: Rosa Montero
(Not Translated)

Zarza awakens, on an ordinary, routine day, in her lowly home, to a phone call. That call returns her to her former life, to the center of the inferno, in a 24 hour race that doesn't allow us to leave the book until we have traversed the entire history of Zarza's hellish past.
Martha Berman, Professor of Language and Literature

El coronel no tiene quien le escriba. *(No One Writes to the Colonel)*
Author: Gabriel García Márquez
(Translated)

The second novel of the Colombian Nobel prize winner narrates the vain hopes of a Colonel, who every Friday awaits an official letter in reply to his justified claim for a pension. The internal tension of the novel arises from the juxtaposition of minutely described daily miseries and the stoical optimism of the main character.
 Juan Pablo Debesis, Lectorum

Cortos. *(Shorts: Stories)*
Author: Alberto Fuguet
(Translated)

In this collection of stories, the Chilean writer Alberto Fuguet accomplished one thing: making clear that one of the unmistakable signs of young Hispanic-American generations is the desire for flight, the wish to disappear. Notoriously watering in the cinema and American pop culture, the Chilean writer reproduces its language, its situations and its mannerisms, as well as in the more fortunate cases, a certain unpredictable character. With its fleeting subject matter, *Shorts* (*Cortos*) should be read today, right now, because it's possible that the world it describes might disappear tomorrow.
 Gaspar Orozco, Mexican Poet and Diplomat

Crack: instrucciones de uso. *(Crack: Directions for Use)*
Author: Ricardo Chávez Castañeda
(Not Translated)

Compilation of a new Mexican literary generation's work, with prologue.
Lynn Shirey, Harvard College Library

El Cristo feo. *(The Ugly Christ)*
Author: Alicia Yañez Cossío
(Not Translated)

Ordalisa, a domestic worker, suffers the whims of her employers, a snooty couple, until she hears a voice in her humble room which inspires her to carve a wooden Christ and to value the worth of her own life.
Richard Heyer, Instituto Cervantes New York

Las crónicas del sochantre. *(The Chronicles of Sochantre)*
Author: Álvaro Cunqueiro
(Not Translated)

As cronicas do Sochantre, along with Merlín e familia and Si o vello Sinbad volvese ás illas, form part of a trilogy which contains the most fabulous and fantastic part of the beautiful world dreamt into existence by Alvaro Cunqueiro. The protagonist of this novel is Charles Anne Guenolè Mathiey de Crozon, better known as Sochantre de Pontivy, born in the year 1772, in the villa of Josslin, on the banks of the river Oust, in French Brittany. Returning to attend the funeral of a gentleman of that locality, Sochantre shares a carriage with a group of strange travelers, all dead and also relatives of the deceased, whose burial they've come to witness.
🔖 *Xosé Luis García Canido, Instituto Cervantes*

Los cuadernos de don Rigoberto. *(The Notebooks of Don Rigoberto)*
Author: Mario Vargas Llosa
(Translated)

Don Rigoberto escapes into fantasies, many of them sexual, by writing in his notebook. This work is not for everyone but I found it intriguing.
🔖 *Millie Torrance, Sacramento Public Library*

El cuarto de atrás. *(The Back Room)*
Author: Carmen Martín Gaite
(Translated)

An oneiric novel that examines the process of writing fiction.
🔖 *Lynn Shirey, Harvard College Library*

Cuentitos simpáticos: A Graded Reader for Advanced Beginning Students.
(Congenial Stories: A Leveled Reader for Advanced Beginners)
Author: Rubin Pfeiffer
(Not Translated)

This book shows several short stories appropriate for the elementary school student. Even when the focus is on the reading, the grammar also plays an important role too. They are short and easy to comprehend and they open the door for a short discussion in class.
🔖 *Guillermina Raffo Magnasco, St. Thomas University*

El cuento hispánico: A Graded Literary Anthology.
(Hispanic Short Stories: A Leveled Literary Anthology)
Author: Edward J. Mullen, and John E. Garganigo
(Not Translated)

These short stories are written by Latin American and Spanish authors, and they contain comprehension exercises aimed at improving students' reading skills.
🔖 *Guillermina Raffo Magnasco, St Thomas University*

Cuentos completos. *(The Complete Stories)*
Author: Julio Cortázar
(Not Translated)

Using the English short story tradition as a point of departure, Julio Cortázar—along with Jorge Luis Borges—made the short story in Spanish a very serious matter, literarily speaking. The literary innovation begun by Cortázar in both traditional time and the linear recitation of a story are ruptured, started a revolution which has become widely accepted and used in literature in Spanish ever since. However, Cortázar's short narratives are not limited to a renovation of styles and forms; each one of them, sometimes catalyzed by the quotidian, presents a fascinating and cinematographic story.
🔖 *Lluís Agustí, Instituto Cervantes New York*

Cuentos completos. *(The Complete Stories)*
Author: Silvina Ocampo
(Not Translated)

The youngest of the Ocampo sisters was not only a poet but an excellent writer of short stories, as was her husband, Adolfo Bioy Casares. Her stories are tragic, somber, full of ghostly figures and told with a certain touch of sadism or a spirit of perversion. They are a must-read.
🔖 *Lluís Agustí, Instituto Cervantes New York*

Cuentos completos (1968-2002). *(The Complete Stories (1968-2002))*
Author: José Agustín
(Not Translated)

A compilation of one of Mexico's most important contemporary authors.
🔖 *Teresa Chapa, University of North Carolina at Chapel Hill*

Los de abajo. *(The Underdogs: A Novel of the Mexican Revolution)*
Author: Mariano Azuela
(Translated)

Azuela's novel was one of the first to tackle the Mexican Revolution, and we can also say, one of the best and most truthful contemporary accounts, a magnificent portrait of a people and an era. The narrative of the military campaign and the personal experience of Demetrio Macías serves as a paradigm of the Mexican who lives, suffers, and fights in the Revolution, sometimes without a clear notion of motives, but impelled by forces beyond his control.
Lluís Agustí, Instituto Cervantes New York

Delirio. *(Delirium)*
Author: Laura Restrepo
(Translated)

Winner of the Premio Alfaguara de novela in 2004, the plot revolves around Aguilar, an unemployed professor, and his search for his missing wife. Set in Restrepo's native Colombia, the novel elicits the country's tropes of drug dealing and money laundering but also explores the daily lives of people struggling to survive.
David Block, Cornell University

El delirio de Turing. *(Turing's Delirium)*
Author: Edmundo Paz Soldán
(Translated)

Paz Soldán uses the world of computer hacking to explore the stuggle between oppressed and oppressor. As he works to crack the codes in what has become an information war, Miguel Sáenz, who has taken the nom de guerre of Turing, discovers that his allies are seriously compromised. Winner of Bolivia's Premio Nacional de Novela in 2002.
David Block, Cornell University

Los detectives salvajes. *(The Savage Detectives)*
Author: Roberto Bolaño
(Translated)

One of the few recent attempts to create the great and total novel in the Spanish language.
José María Conget, Writer

Distinguida Señora. *(Honorable Madam)*
Author: Carmen Imbert Brugal
(Not Translated)

This novel takes place in a transitional period from tyranny to democracy following the death of dictator Rafael Trujillo in the Dominican Republic. It is a time of historical confusion where there is breakdown of social and moral values, giving birth to feminist liberalism. It tells the story of a woman in search of life's pleasures within a spurious social legitimacy.
🖜 *Sarah Aponte, Dominican Studies Institute. CUNY*

Don Quijote de la Mancha. *(Don Quixote)*
Author: Miguel de Cervantes
(Translated)

What can one say about everyone's idealistic hero and his faithful sidekick. Always popular and studied in Spanish and literature classes and in translation, this classic should be read and re-read at different stages of one's life.
🖜 *Millie Torrance, Sacramento Public Library*

En busca del unicornio. *(In Search of the Unicorn)*
Author: Juan Eslava Galán
(Not Translated)

King Henry IV of Castile, called the Impotent, needs help to ensure that his lineage will keep the throne. To accomplish this, he sends one of his best knights, Juan de Olid, in search of a unicorn's horn, in the hope that the horn's aphrodisiac effects will help the monarch with his task. The knight departs for the heart of Africa in search of the mythical animal accompanied by a small and unique contingent which include a friar and a virgin girl, who, according to legend, must be offered in order to attract the elusive animal. A hilarious and entertaining parody of historical and adventure novels.
🖜 *Lluís Agustí, Instituto Cervantes New York*

En el último azul. *(In the Last Blue)*
Author: Carme Riera
(Translated)

The Mallorcan writer Carme Riera obtained the National Literature Prize granted annually by the Spanish Ministry of Culture for this novel, one of the best ever written about the crypto-Jews of Spain and about the last great Inquisitorial

LITERATURE / FICTION ●

trials. Set in the 17th century, the novel is based on, sad to say, real events which took place in Palma de Mallorca. A group of *xuetes* (name by which the descendants of Mallorcan Jews were derisively known) prepares to flee toward Leghorn by sea, with its blue promise of liberty. A novel which depicts the religious intransigence of an era, but which also serves as a reflection on current attitudes. An excellent novel, beautifully written and recently translated into English.
🔊 *Lluís Agustí, Instituto Cervantes New York*

El entenado. *(The Witness)*
Author: Juan José Saer
(Translated)

A journey to the beginnings of civilization and also a reflection on «otherness», on another language and way of life. A man who lived among Indians for ten years, and now as an old man, recounts his life.
🔊 *Martha Berman, Professor of Language and Literature*

Entre visillos. *(Behind the Curtains)*
Author: Carmen Martín Gaite
(Translated)

Premio Nadal 1957.
🔊 *Patricia Figueroa, Brown University Library*

Escuela de mandarines. *(School of Mandarins)*
Author: Miguel Espinosa
(Not Translated)

A classic of the Spanish Baroque written in the middle of the 20th century. A forgotten genius from Murcia, who in my judgment wrote the most important work of Spanish literature since *Don Quixote*.
🔊 *Juan Carlos Vidal, Instituto Cervantes Chicago*

El estadio de mármol. *(The Marble Stadium)*
Author: Juan Bonilla
(Not Translated)

The best, to my mind, collection of stories by a young Spanish author.
🔊 *José María Conget, Writer*

Eva Luna. *(Eva Luna)*
Author: Isabel Allende
(Translated)

When a text like Eva Luna's adventures can carry you out of the shadows of a snowy, wintery week North of Chicago, it has a place in everyone's shelf.
🔊 *Adan Griego, Stanford University Libraries*

La familia de Pascual Duarte. *(The Family of Pacual Duarte)*
Author: Camilo José Cela
(Translated)

This was the first novel of Nobel laureate Camilo José Cela and most translated of his long career. Naturalist in style, it relates with no holds barred the ruthless life of a murderer, a peasant from Extremadura by the name of Pascual Duarte. Although there is a constant state of alarm throughout the work and a savage tone which causes one to shudder, there is a certain lyricism in Duarte's personality, in spite of the brutality of his actions, he seems more of a victim of circumstances than their catalyst. The sensation which the novel caused outside of Spain seems to suggest that Pascual Duarte may be the confirmation of the Spanish topoi of violence and bloodthirstiness.
🔊 *Lluís Agustí, Instituto Cervantes New York*

Farabeuf. *(Farabeuf)*
Author: Salvador Elizondo
(Translated)

An avant-garde novel in which narrative time and the broadest perspectivism possible are completely suspended. It forms part of that opening toward the East embraced by other Mexican authors such as Octavio Paz and Sergio Pitol. A unique gem of the literary avant-garde in the world of Hispanic letters.
🔊 *Juan Carlos Vidal, Instituto Cervantes Chicago*

Felices días, tío Sergio. *(Happy Days, Uncle Sergio)*
Author: Magali García Ramis
(Translated)

In search of her cultural identity, the protagonist of this novel paints a picture of a hopeful Puerto Rico during the Muñoz Marín era. The author addresses weighty themes for the times (the independence movement, machismo, homosexuality) in a simple yet mature literary style.
🔊 *Sabrina Abreu, Instituto Cervantes New York*

Ficciones. *(Collected Fictions)*
Author: Jorge Luis Borges
(Translated)

In this essential compilation of some of Borges' best short stories such as, *Tlö, Uqbar, Orbis Tertius, La biblioteca de Babel* and *La lotería en Babilonia,* the reader will encounter several of the themes that appear in many of Borges' works such as treachery, mirrors, loneliness, folk heroes, out of this world and the universe.
🔊 *Alvaro Sanabria, San Francisco Public Library*

La fiesta del Chivo. *(The Feast of the Goat)*
Author: Mario Vargas Llosa
(Translated)

Peruvian novelist and essayist, Mario Vargas Llosa, is one of Latin-American leading writers. In *The Feast of the Goat*, he recreates the final days of Dominican Republic dictator General Rafael Trujillo's evil regime.
🔊 *Libbhy Romero, Brooklyn Public Library*

La forja de un rebelde. *(The Forging of a Rebel)*
Author: Arturo Barea
(Translated)

A fundamental work to understand 20th century Spain. It consists of three autobiographical novels which cover his childhood and adolescence in Madrid, his military service in Morocco, and conclude with the Civil War years, illuminating the entire era.
🔊 *Richard Heyer, Instituto Cervantes New York*

Fortunata y Jacinta: dos historias de casadas.
(Fortunata and Jacinta: Two Stories of Married Women)
Author: Benito Pérez Galdós
(Translated)

A classic 19th century novel set in Madrid, this is a thoroughly enjoyable tale full of politics and social customs of the period.
🔊 *Lynn Shirey, Harvard College Library*

Galíndez. *(Galíndez)*
Author: Manuel Vázquez Montalbán
(Translated)

Exiled in the Dominican Republic after the Spanish Civil war, the Basque nationalist politician Jesús de Galíndez collaborated with the Dominican government. Later he moved to New York as representative of the Basque government in exile and perhaps as a CIA informant. At Columbia University he starts to work on a book about the inner workings of the Trujillo dictatorship. The secret police of the Dominican dictator kidnapped Galíndez in Manhattan in 1956 and transferred him to the island, where he was tortured and killed. An American woman investigates his disappearance in the 1980's.
🔊 *Lluís Agustí, Instituto Cervantes New York*

Los girasoles ciegos. *(Blind Sunflowers)*
Author: Alberto Méndez
(Not Translated)

Four exceptional stories, posthumously published, by a 60 year old first-time author, who would never know the far-reaching effects of the quality of his work.
🔊 *José María Conget, Writer*

La guaracha del Macho Camacho. *(Macho Camacho's Beat)*
Author: Luis Rafael Sánchez
(Translated)

With this work, Sánchez revolutionizes the Puerto Rican novel, bringing to light the musical and vertiginous rhythm of his people.
🔊 *Sabrina Abreu, Instituto Cervantes New York*

Guzmán de Alfarache. *(The Rogue, or The Life of Guzman de Alfarache)*
Author: Mateo Alemán
(Translated)

A masterpiece of the picaresque genre, this novel is remarkable not only for its vivid narration of adventures and its philosophical observations, but also for its evocation of the life, morals and manners of the period of the Counter Reformation in Spain and Italy.
🔊 *Eduardo de Lamadrid, Trans-Lingual Communications Inc.*

El hablador. *(The Storyteller)*
Author: Mario Vargas Llosa
(Translated)

An intriguing fable about an indigenous people in Peru's Amazon, and the white storyteller who crosses cultural boundaries.
🔊 *Lynn Shirey, Harvard College Library*

Hasta el fin de los cuentos. *(Until Stories End)*
Author: José María Conget
(Not Translated)

One of the principal characteristics of José María Conget's work, author for a happy few, is its humanity, especially in some of its more interesting manifestations, humor and curiosity. Coupled to this trait is an extensive knowledge of literature (both *good* and *bad*) and film. *Hasta el fin de los cuentos* is a magnificent compendium of tales about and for literature, a profound and beautiful book which is read with the ease of someone joined in hand to another who knows the way perfectly.
🔊 *Lluís Agustí, Instituto Cervantes New York*

Hasta no verte, Jesús mío. *(Here's to You, Jesusa!)*
Author: Elena Poniatowska
(Translated)

Journalist and author Poniatowska based this testimonial novel on a series of interviews conducted with an indigenous woman who recounted her difficult struggle to survive in modern-day Mexico.
🔊 *Teresa Chapa, University of North Carolina at Chapel Hill*

Helena o el mar del verano. *(Helena or the Summer Sea)*
Author: Julián Ayesta
(Not Translated)

Julián Ayesta's brief, lyrical, and exquisite evocation of memories of summer vacations during childhood. While Ayesta was not a prolific nor a successful author, this is without a doubt one of the most beatiful novels of childhood in Spanish literature of the 20th century.
🔊 *Lluís Agustí, Instituto Cervantes New York*

Herencia: The Anthology of Hispanic Literature of the United States.
Author: Nicolas Kanellos, ed.
(Bilingual)

Excellent Spanish/English collection of U.S. Hispanic stories!
 Christine Peterson, Marantha Academy

Hermana muerte. *(Sister Death)*
Author: Justo Navarro
(Not Translated)

Perhaps the best crafted novel by one of the best Spanish writers of recent generations, capable of creating a disturbing hard-boiled world seen through a lyrical gaze, in a refined language where the character expresses the innermost basis of their actions.
Ernesto Pérez Zúñiga, Instituto Cervantes

Herrumbrosas lanzas. *(Rusty Spears)*
Author: Juan Benet
(Not Translated)

This pentad represents Juan Benet's best work and, in my opinion, the best work ever written about the Spanish Civil War. A perfect symbiosis of a frame of reference and a decadent atmosphere from which emerges all the complexity of the human psyche.
Juan Carlos Vidal, Instituto Cervantes Chicago

La higuera. *(The Fig Tree)*
Author: Ramiro Pinilla
(Not Translated)

Many of us who have been devoted followers since we discovered the existence of literature back in the 60's -when we used to pass from hand to hand books edited by Pinilla in Libropueblo editions- are stunned by the phenomenon of Pinilla. In later years he has not only rewritten his monumental *Green Valleys, Red Hills* (*Verdes valles, colinas rojas*, 3 vol. Tusquets, 2005-2006), the first volume of which was first published in the 80's and which now culminates in this excellent trilogy, but also now offers us a surprising work called *The Fig Tree* (*La Higuera*), Set in his native Getxo, Pinilla creates a narrative centered on the thorny theme of political reprisals in the aftermath of the Civil War. The relation between the protagonist, a Falangist and author of the reprisals, and a boy, child of the victims, serves as the framework in which to brilliantly expose the irrationality of those years, which today we wish were prehistoric. We are fortunate to have this new offering by Ramiro Pinilla, a writer who is currently enjoying overdue recognition, after having received the Euskadi Prize for the Novel in 2005, the Critic's Award in 2005 and the National Narrative Award in 2006.

🔊 *Miguel Valladares, Dartmouth College*

Hijo de ladrón. *(Son of a Thief)*
Author: Manuel Rojas
(Not Translated)

The adventures of Aniceto Hevia, the son of a thief («hijo de ladrón») and protagonist of this novel is clearly a major achievement in mid-20th-century Chilean social literature. Writer Manuel Rojas did not need to probe his imagination or creativity to create his novels and short stories: an attentive ear for reproducing popular speech and a concern for putting day-to-day experiences down on paper was enough. Yet this novel surpasses all that, ensuring that *Hijo de ladrón*, its protagonist and Rojas' fiction overall become more than mere genre work, and transforming the most simple and local material into beautiful literature.

🔊 *Lluís Agustí, Instituto Cervantes New York*

Hijos sin hijos. *(Sons Without Sons)*
Author: Enrique Vila-Matas
(Not Translated)

Audacious, unique and heterodox novel which could be interpreted as a «Brief History of Spain» in the second half of the 20th century. The protagonists of the various episodes are all sons without sons; persons who do not wish to have descendants, beings whose own nature distances them from society and who do not need help of any kind.

🔊 *Paloma Celis Carbajal, UW-Madison*

Hipotermia. *(Hypothermia)*
Author: Álvaro Enrigue
(Not Translated)

Hypothermia is a fragmentary novel comprised of seemingly unconnected stories, but whose common denominator is the shocking and strange way which the narrator shifts his gaze over environments and situations which are equally fractured and inapprehensible. In part a product of his stay in the capital city of the United States, this effective exercise dissects the characters and antiheroes of everyday life, thereby allowing Álvaro Enrigue (1969) to deploy the narrative tools and instruments of the efficient and impassive scrutinizer of existences and ruins.

🔊 *Bruno Hernández Piché, Mexican Writer and Diplomat*

Historia de un abrigo. *(History of a Coat)*
Author: Soledad Puértolas
(Not Translated)

A novel where numerous stories get intersected when the main character starts to look for her mother's coat. A look at the complexity of family relations.
🔍 *Patricia Figueroa, Brown University Library*

Historia de una gaviota y del gato que le enseñó a volar.
(The Story of a Seagull and the Cat Who Taught Her to Fly)
Author: Luis Sepúlveda
(Translated)

Nothing is more charming than this story for kids aged 8 to 88. Our big, fat, sweet cat finds a gull on the roof of a house when the owner is on vacation. The gull asks the cat to care for her egg until it hatches and to teach the hatchling how to fly, since she is about to die from the effects of an oil slick. Guess who helps the cat with this mission. A beautiful and poetic story.
🔍 *Martha Berman, Professor of Language and Literature*

Historias de cronopios y de famas. *(Cronopios and Famas)*
Author: Julio Cortázar
(Translated)

A collection of short stories by one of Latin America's most important writers. Cortázar offers satirical observations on human character in these humoristic tales.
🔍 *Teresa Chapa, University of North Carolina at Chapel Hill*

Imán. *(Magnet)*
Author: Ramón J. Sender
(Not Translated)

Imán was the first novel by the prolific Spanish writer Ramón J. Sender, exiled in the United States. A fictional retelling of his own experiences as a military physician during the Moroccan War, Spain's colonial war against the tribes of the Rif in the 1920's, the novel addresses the military incompetence and corruption of the Spanish army in Africa, and the atrocities of the campaign are related in a critical and realist style.
🔍 *Lluís Agustí, Instituto Cervantes New York*

Incierta gloria. *(Uncertain Glory)*
Author: Joan Sales
(Not Translated)

Taken from a line of William Shakespeare, «The uncertain glory of an April day», the title of this novel, to my taste one of the best, and concomitantly perhaps one the least known about Civil War, alludes to the proclamation of the Second Spanish Republic in April 1931. Constantly rewritten by its author, it was first published in a censored version in Spain, and then was published whole in French and in exile. Three characters and a War, that functions not as a setting but rather as a protagonist, with its interminable times of suspense at an inactive front, in lower Aragon, make room somehow for love and reflection. It includes descriptions of the struggles between communists and anarchists, the bombings of cities and the rebellions of the rearguard, the dispersion of 1939 and the sad and desolate aftermath.
🔍 *Lluís Agustí, Instituto Cervantes New York*

El Indio. *(El Indio)*
Author: Gregorio López y Fuentes
(Translated)

Story of a nameless tribe of Indians living in the mountains of Mexico. A timeless tale of the manners and customs that have all but disappeared.
🔍 *Angélica Hurtado-Gracia, LAPL*

Indios en rebelión. *(The Indian Revolt)*
Author: Néstor Taboada Terán
(Not Translated)

The short-story collection *Indios en rebelión* is one of Bolivian writer Néstor Taboada Terán's best-known works. The narrative core of these stories—presented in a style that seems to branch in many directions—revolves around political and social events in mid-20th-century Bolivia.
🔍 *Lluís Agustí, Instituto Cervantes New York*

Industrias y andanzas de Alfanhuí.
(The Adventures of the Ingenious Alfanhuí)
Author: Rafael Sánchez Ferlosio
(Translated)

Expelled from school, a child named Alfanhuí travels throughout Castile and comes to understand reality in an extraordinary and fantastic manner. Sánchez

Ferlosio's clean, poetic and inimitable style in this novel will impress and surprise readers from the first sentence on, and will not abandon nor tire them. A small literary gem upon which time has been unable to make inroads.
 Lluís Agustí, Instituto Cervantes New York

Las inquietudes de Shanti Andía. *(The Restlessness of Shanti Andía)*
Author: Pío Baroja
(Translated)

The action novel *The restlessness of Shanti Andía* forms part of Pío Baroja's trilogy *The Sea (El mar)*, and has been a staple in the reading lists of many generations of Spanish youth and adolescents. It relates the adventures of Juan de Aguirre, a Basque sailor, and the uncle of Shanti Andia and the pirate Zaldumbide.
 Lluís Agustí, Instituto Cervantes New York

La invención de Morel. *(Invention of Morel and Other Stories)*
Author: Adolfo Bioy Casares
(Translated)

A fugitive narrates the imaginary and incredible story of tourists who arrive at the island where he is hiding out. The triangle formed by the scientist Morel, Faustine and the fugitive himself functions as a way of speculating on love and immortality. *La invención de Morel* is a fantastical, extraordinary work, perhaps Bioy Casares's best. With a prologue by his friend and partner in literary adventure, Jorge Luis Borges.
 Lluís Agustí, Instituto Cervantes New York

El invierno en Lisboa. *(Winter in Lisbon)*
Author: Antonio Muñoz Molina
(Translated)

An intriguing thriller. *Lynn Shirey, Harvard College Library*

El jinete polaco. *(The Polish Horseman)*
Author: Antonio Muñoz Molina
(Not Translated)

The best work of one of Spain's most important contemporary novelists.
Lynn Shirey, Harvard College Library

El juguete rabioso. *(Mad Toy)*
Author: Roberto Arlt
(Translated)

A hybrid of the picaresque and existential novel, and taking violence, anguish and the impossibility of progress or redemption as thematic elements, Arlt's novel relates the formative years of Silvio Astier, which are marked by misery and by a series of constant errors and failures, that in the aggregate, constitute his life.
🔊 *Lluís Agustí, Instituto Cervantes New York*

Juventud en éxtasis. *(Juventud en éxtasis)*
Author: Carlos Cuauhtémoc Sánchez
(Not Translated)

A highly acclaimed author who provides his audience with fictional situations about problems teenagers will encounter in real life, and how to deal with them. The resolutions are not heavy handed and are meant for both teenagers and parents to learn how to deal with sexuality.
🔊 *Angela Encinas, San Bernardino Public Library*

El lápiz del carpintero. *(The Carpenter's Pencil)*
Author: Manuel Rivas
(Translated)

Among authors writing in Galician, Manuel Rivas is one of the most well-known outside his native Galicia. *The Carpenter's Pencil* recounts the relationship between a prison guard, Herbal, and a physician, Daniel Da Barca, during the Civil War in Galicia. Dr. Da Barca is imprisoned because of his ideas and has fallen in love with Marisa Mallo, a daughter of the regime. Herbal is jealous of the doctor and avails himself of the pencil of a carpenter who had been shot in the temple. A magnificent literary work with an element of the magical.
🔊 *Lluís Agustí, Instituto Cervantes New York*

El Lazarillo de Tormes. *(The Life of Lazarillo de Tormes)*
Author: Anonymous
(Translated)

This is one of the classics of Spanish literature. Its searing social commentary may sometimes prove frightening to the reader, but at the same time it reflects the atmosphere of the age with more than a modicum of realism. Moreover, Lazarillo himself is such a strong and unforgettable character that he has become the archetypal anti-hero.
🔊 *Mark Pendleton, Branigan Library Las Cruces NM*

El lector novohispano. *(A New Spain Reader)*
Author: José Joaquín Blanco, ed.
(Not Translated)

The Mexican novelist and essayist José Joaquín Blanco (Mexico City, 1951) has compiled in this volume the central poetical, narrative, theatrical and historical texts of the viceroyalty of New Spain, thereby rescuing an epoch of literary and cultural vigor and artistry which has been unjustly forgotten, and which becomes essential for a full understanding of today's Mexico. In the introductory essay, Blanco offers the reader an overview of the literary output of New Spain and its major figures, giving them the due truly owed to them because of their historical and literary value.

🔊 *Gaspar Orozco, Mexican Poet and Diplomat*

Libro del Caballero Zifar. *(Book of the Knight Zifar)*
Author: Anonymous
(Translated)

The oldest Spanish romance of chivalry, written between 1299 and 1305. The work is a medley containing adaptations of saints lives, popular tales, adventures of knight errantry, miraculous ocurrences. The knight errantry of Zifar and his sons, and the episode of the Lady in the Lake are conceived in the spirit of Arthurian legends. El Ribaldo, squire to one of Zifar's sons, is a kind of forerunner to Sancho Panza, and introduces a refreshing note of picaresque realism and self-mockery.

🔊 *Eduardo de Lamadrid, Trans-Lingual Communications Inc.*

El libro del Conde Lucanor. *(Book of Count Lucanor)*
Author: Juan Manuel, Infante de Castilla
(Translated)

El Conde Lucanor is Don Juan Manuel's great 14th century masterpiece, a collection of 50 moral tales or «exempla» in the style of Boccacio's *Decameron*, but anticipating it by more than a decade. The frame is provided by Count Lucanor's problems and his counselor Patronio's solutions, each in the form of a tale ending with a rhymed moral. The tales are composed in a lucid, informal and spirited style that set the standard for the age, and is relevant to our own.

🔊 *Eduardo de Lamadrid, Trans-Lingual Communications Inc.*

Los libros arden mal. *(Books Burn Badly)*
Author: Manuel Rivas
(Not Translated)

Narrative about the persecution of people and ideas in La Coruña during the Franco era, it recounts the burning of the books of the private library of Casares Quiroga, making reference to the minister, his wife and above all, his daughter, already a celebrated actress with the National Theater of Paris. In my opinion, this is a very good book because it skillfully combines history and fiction, leaving the reader with a bitter taste and a sense of the great injustice of Francoism, against ideas and persons, killing many and persecuting others.
🔊 *Carmen de Zulueta, Writer and Professor*

Lo fugitivo permanece. 20 cuentos mexicanos.
(The Permanence of the Impermanent: 20 Mexican Stories)
Author: Carlos Monsiváis, ed.
(Not Translated)

Selection of stories by nineteen Mexican writers published between 1934-1984. This anthology provides a representative sample of achievements and tendencies, of characters and customs from an era which witnessed the transformation of traditional Mexico into modern Mexico. The writers included in this anthology are: Juan de la Cabada, José Revueltas, Edmundo Valadés, Juan José Arreola, Elena Garro, Augusto Monterroso, Ricardo Garibay, Jorge Ibargüengoitia, Carlos Fuentes, Juan García Ponce, Juan Vicente Melo, Sergio Pitol, Elena Poniatowska, Eraclio Zepeda, José Emilio Pachecho, José Agustín, Héctor Aguilar Camín, Guillermo Samperio, Juan Villoro.
🔊 *Paloma Celis Carbajal, UW-Madison*

Lo que está en mi corazón. *(In My Heart)*
Author: Marcela Serrano
(Not Translated)

This is both, a self discovery novel and a political one set in Chiapas, Mexico. I found it well written with wonderful descriptions of San Cristobal and an intriguing look at «zapatism».
🔊 *Millie Torrance, Sacramento Public Library*

Llámame Brooklyn. *(Call Me Brooklyn)*
Author: Eduardo Lago
(Not translated)

Call Me Brooklyn by Eduardo Lago is a novel whose complex narrative structure obeys the peculiarities of a tale with multiple ramifications in which a love story, a confused identity and an artistic adventure are incessantly interspersed through several moments in time and place which constitute a personal geography. Spain and North America, Europe and the American continents unite and separate to allow a profound and rigorous reflection about the very act of writing the novel which we are reading, and which, at the same time, we will never come to know. An intensely Spanish and Cervantine text which could only have been written outside of Spain.
🔊 *Isaías Lerner, CUNY*

La lluvia amarilla. *(The Yellow Rain)*
Author: Julio Llamazares
(Translated)

La lluvia amarilla is the story of the death of a town in the province of Huesca in the Pyrenees as told by the last of its inhabitants, Andrés de Casa Sosas, a sick and lonely old man who during the last day of his life sees, in a kind of hallucination, some of the characters of the village which has witnessed his birth and now his death.
🔊 *Lluís Agustí, Instituto Cervantes New York*

El mal mundo. *(Bad World)*
Author: Luis Antonio de Villena
(Not Translated)

To portray the desire for the other, the other like you, and have that sameness with a discourse of no shame or guilt, that's the liberating text of Villena. *El mal mundo* won the Erotic Literary Prize of La Sonrisa Vertical in 1999.
🔊 *Adan Griego, Stanford University Libraries*

Mala onda. *(Bad Vibes)*
Author: Alberto Fuguet
(Translated)

A coming of age novel set in Chile as Pinochet's dictatorship is confronting growing opposition.
🔊 *Teresa Chapa, University of North Carolina at Chapel Hill*

Materia prima: protonovela. *(Raw Material: A Protonovela)*
Author: Marcio Veloz Maggiolo
(Not Translated)

The story is told through the life of Ariel, who upon returning to Santo Domingo, finds himself with the task of complying with the dying wish of his friend Persio. Persio turns over letters, interviews, notes and drafts of chapters to Ariel and charges him with writing and publishing the novel which the former wasn't able nor will be able to create. This *Raw Material* will make Ariel confront the past, from which the not very pleasant experiences of the neighborhood's inhabitants during the years of the Trujillo will resurface. A kind of magic envelops the characters and the city and creates a complex story.
🔖 *Sarah Aponte, Dominican Studies Institute. CUNY*

Melodrama. *(Melodrama)*
Author: Jorge Franco
(Not Translated)

Vidal, a handsome young man, one day discovers a mark on his neck that is the warning of a fatal illness. Since he's not able to tell Perla the disgrace, he abandons her. He prefers that she make false suppositions. It seems that Vidal dies soon and his condition as an omniscient dead man allows him to tell us about his life and family. But Vidal isn't dead and his relationship with Perla isn't what we believe it to be at the beginning. The unravelling of the intrigue happens in small doses that keeps us on edge for nearly 400 pages.
🔖 *Tom LaSalle, Ferguson Library*

Memorias de Altagracia. *(Memories of Altagracia)*
Author: Salvador Garmendia
(Translated)

Salvador Garmendia is one of the most interesting novelists to come out of Venezuela in the 20th century. As García Márquez does with Macondo, Garmendia makes *Memorias de Altagracia* into a marvelous nostalgic journey through childhood and the rural world that disappears in adulthood, which he tries to preserve in this work.
🔖 *Lluís Agustí, Instituto Cervantes New York*

Milagros de Nuestra Señora. *(Miracles of Our Lady)*
Author: Gonzalo de Berceo
(Translated)

Berceo is the earliest known poet in Spanish literature and the first representative of the «mester de clerecía» school. This great religious poem, presented as a collection of 25 tales, is written is an intimate, personal style. Berceo interspersed

his narrative with simple humor and realistic homely detail which accentuate his at times almost mystical reverence. His populism and rustic language continue to exercise their spell and charm the modern reader. His other best known work is a vivid account of the life of Santo Domingo de Silos.
🔊 *Eduardo de Lamadrid, Trans-Lingual Communications Inc.*

El misterio de la cripta embrujada. *(The Mystery of the Enchanted Crypt)*
Author: Eduardo Mendoza
(Not Translated)

A very satiric, gothic novel set in Barcelona. 🔊 *Lynn Shirey, Harvard College Library*

Misteriosa Buenos Aires. *(Mysterious Buenos Aires)*
Author: Manuel Mújica Láinez
(Not Translated)

By means of a series of chronologically arranged stories, the Argentine writer Mújica Láinez reconstructs the history of Buenos Aires since its foundation to the 20th century. An exquisite reconstruction of characters and epochs through the superb gifts for narrative and evocation by the author of another of the greatest novels in Spanish of all time, *Bomarzo*.
🔊 *Lluís Agustí, Instituto Cervantes New York*

La muerte de Artemio Cruz. *(The Death of Artemio Cruz)*
Author: Carlos Fuentes
(Translated)

Mexican novelist Fuentes narrates the events of Artemio Cruz's life on his death bed in various voices. One reviewer wrote that before dying Cruz examines the value of his existence.
🔊 *Millie Torrance, Sacramento Public Library*

La mujer del maestro. *(The Teacher's Wife)*
Author: Guillermo Martínez
(Not Translated)

Picks up the literature of relationships and feelings where Benedetti [*The Respite (La tregua)*, the interesting Benedetti] and Onetti [*The Goodbyes (Los adioses)*, *As Sad as Her (Tan triste como ella)*, etc] left off, although never sufficiently explored due to the hyper-politicized of our literature. This short novel is written in a simple and elegant Spanish which recalls the masters of the Generation of 1898.
🔊 *Mónica Flores-Correa, Professor and Writer*

Mujeres de ojos grandes. *(Women with Big Eyes)*
Author: Ángeles Mastretta
(Translated)

Set in Puebla, Mexico, the stories recount the traditions and lives of Mexican women in past decades.
📢 *Millie Torrance, Sacramento Public Library*

El mundo alucinante. *(Hallucinations)*
Author: Reinaldo Arenas
(Translated)

This is the story of one amazing character, the candid and picaresque Fray Servando, a Latin American hero who finds himself fighting against the Spanish Inquisition during the time of the Mexican independence wars. The novel is a dialogue between fiction and history, fantasy and magic, where some events are told from several perspectives. A whimsical, amazing read.
📢 *Alina San Juan, Trade Comission of Spain*

Nada. *(Nada)*
Author: Carmen Laforet
(Translated)

A feminist novel about a yound woman who moves to Barcelona to study in the wake of the Spanish Civil War.
📢 *Patricia Figueroa, Brown University Library*

Nadie encendía las lámparas y otros cuentos.
(When the Lamps Remained Unlit and Other Stories)
Author: Felisberto Hernández
(Not Translated)

One of the best short stories collections in Latin American literature of all time. These stories are a wonder of magic, mystery and poetry. Anticipates the aesthetics of current short story writing.
📢 *Eduardo Lago, Instituto Cervantes New York*

Niebla. *(Mist: a Tragicomic Novel)*
Author: Miguel de Unamuno
(Translated)

A key work in Spanish literature. In this novel, Unamuno tackles once again the golden theme of the ambiguity between reality and fiction, and combines it with the narrative innovation of dialogues between the creator and his characters.
◗ *Paloma Celis Carbajal, UW-Madison*

No será la tierra. *(It Won't Be the Earth)*
Author: Jorge Volpi
(Not Translated)

This novel narrates the great transformations of our time: the fall of the Berlin Wall, the coup d'etat against Gorbachev, Yeltsin's ascension to power, germ warfare and the Human Genome Project. In a style both elegant and profound, Volpi explores the avarice, the passion and the egotism which move human beings, within the political-historical context of globalization.
◗ *Juan Pablo Debesis, Lectorum*

Novelas ejemplares. *(Exemplary Stories)*
Author: Miguel de Cervantes
(Translated)

The best short narratives in the Spanish language. Others probably named *Don Quixote*, the obvious selection. But this volume definitively changed the course of short fiction in the Spanish language and profoundly influenced other European literatures. No subsequent novelist has escaped its influence.
◗ *Isaías Lerner, CUNY*

La novia de Odessa. *(The Bride from Odessa)*
Author: Edgardo Cozarinsky
(Translated)

Relatively unknown until now by the public at large, Edgardo Cozarinsky is an Argentine filmmaker and writer who has resided in Paris since 1974. *The Bride from Odessa* (*La novia de Odessa*) is an excellent work from the literary point of view, combining fiction and memory in a fascinating way. The intertwined personal stories of Cozarinsky's Jewish oral memory leads us to reflect on the meaning and truthfulness of origins and history.
◗ *Lluís Agustí, Instituto Cervantes New York*

La novia oscura. *(The Dark Bride)*
Author: Laura Restrepo
(Translated)

This is one of the best Latin American novels published in the last 20 years. This book has been praised as factual, beautiful, funny, perceptive, luminous an unforgettable.
🔊 *Alvaro Sanabria, San Francisco Public Library*

Nubosidad variable. *(Variable Cloud)*
Author: Carmen Martín Gaite
(Translated)

An intense and intimate contemporary novel about a mature woman's friendship and the nature of writing.
🔊 *Lynn Shirey, Harvard College Library*

Obabakoak. *(Obabakoak: A Novel)*
Author: Bernardo Atxaga
(Translated)

Bernardo Axtaga is among those Basque writers whose work has been recognized and widely disseminated beyond the borders of Eusquera. His best-known is perhaps *Obabakoak*, which received the National Literature Prize granted by the Spanish Ministry of Culture. *Obabakoak* is a collection of finely honed, humorous and ironic short stories. The stories are all set in Obaba, a somewhat magical imaginary region in the Basque country. A magnificent work of universal scope.
🔊 *Lluís Agustí, Instituto Cervantes New York*

Obras completas (y otros cuentos). *(Complete Works & Other Stories)*
Author: Augusto Monterroso
(Translated)

«God has not yet created the world; he is only imagining it, as if he were half asleep. That is why the world is perfect, but confused,» is both the beginning and end of one of Augusto Monterroso's stories. This author's works are always short; they are subtly ironic more than humorous. Better known as Tito, Monterroso—a native of Guatemala—is the reason this literary genre predicated on brevity has achieved maturity in Spanish. A clean and pleasant read, and highly recommended.
🔊 *Lluís Agustí, Instituto Cervantes New York*

El obsceno pájaro de la noche. *(The Obscene Bird of Night)*
Author: José Donoso
(Translated)

The voice which narrates this eminent work from the Latin American boom flows indefatigably from the lips of the Little Mute, as in a voyage from being to nothingness, creating a cavernous and decrepit world. A world which from the first to last page acquires the dimension of a universe from which the reader cannot escape.
🔊 *Juan Pablo Debesis, Lectorum*

Oficina N° 1. *(Oficina N° 1)*
Author: Miguel Otero Silva
(Not Translated)

The work of writer, politician and journalist Otero Silva focuses on human, social and political problems in Venezuela. *Oficina No.1* is an interesting novel about the oil industry in that country.
🔊 *Lluís Agustí, Instituto Cervantes New York*

Ojo por diente. *(Eye for a Tooth)*
Author: Rubén Bareiro Saguier
(Not Translated)

The Paraguayan poet and storyteller Rubén Bareiro offers in this work eleven stories of a social character about the reality as lived in Paraguay. Although this statement may appear superfluous, and perhaps also due to his experiences of persecution and exile, language, the word, assumes pride of place in this book, and in all of Bareiro's work. In his stories flows his poetry, a poetry expressed both in Spanish and Guarani. The resulting multiplicity of sonorous registries allows the poet to delve deeply into language, into all languages, into the formal beauty of words and images. An author that needs to be rediscovered.
🔊 *Lluís Agustí, Instituto Cervantes New York*

Los ojos de Judas y otros cuentos. *(The Eyes of Judas and Other Stories)*
Author: Abraham Valdelomar
(Not Translated)

In evocative and nostalgic stories such as *Carmelo the Gentleman* and *The Eyes of Judas*, the author depicts the life and customs of the port of Pisco at the end of the 19th century. It also includes *Abraham Valdelomar: Life and Work*, a critical study of the author and his work.
🔊 *Richard Heyer, Instituto Cervantes New York*

Operación Hagen. *(Operation Hagen)*
Author: Felipe Botaya
(Not Translated)

I strongly recommend this book since it is a true story, with a profusion of technical detail and information of which I was unaware. The story's setting is finely realized and the characters are well-developed and deep. Truly a rarity in a less than stimulating publishing environment.
 Florencio Bernal, reader

 El oscurecer. *(The Darkening)*
Author: Luis Mateo Díez
(Not Translated)

The wise desolation of old age is depicted in this fable where the real and the symbolic appear magisterially fused in the cereal fields which surround an old train station. Composed as an intimate confidence made to the reader, this is one of the best works in Spanish of the modern era.
Ernesto Pérez Zúñiga, Instituto Cervantes

La otra mano de Lepanto. *(The Other Hand at Lepanto)*
Author: Carmen Boullosa
(Not Translated)

A reformulation in a contemporary key of Cervantes' *Gitanilla* from the *Exemplary Novels* and of the legendary *Battle of Lepanto*, in which the heroine is a combatant aboard the galleon La Real. María the Dancer observes the passage of the century in this intensely literary work, whose pages follow one another in such quick succession that the reader is literally left breathless. This monumental and fortunate novel confirms the Mexican writer as a major novelist of her generation in an international context.
Juan Pablo Debesis, Lectorum

 Una palabra tuya. *(One Word from You)*
Author: Elvira Lindo
(Not Translated)

Winner of the Biblioteca Breve Prize, *Una palabra tuya* narrates the story of a woman who's dissatisfied with the evolution of her life, work, friends and love relationships. Although Elvira Lindo is perhaps best known for her comical children's books, and for the multiple registries her language assumes taken from

popular and everyday speech, in this novel she displays a superior command of language to describe and share pain, to narrate the epic of normal lives, and to show the human tragedy, of taking final responsibility for one's own happiness.
🔖 *Lluís Agustí, Instituto Cervantes New York*

Pantaleón y las visitadoras. *(Captain Pantoja and the Special Service)*
Author: Mario Vargas Llosa
(Translated)

The misfortunes of the honest Captain Pantaleón Pantoja, obliged to organize an army of women to help pacify Peruvian troops in the Amazon jungle, revolutionized the life of the region. A delectable and hilarious novel about efficiency, military devotion, and desire.
🔖 *Lluís Agustí, Instituto Cervantes New York*

Paradiso. *(Paradise)*
Author: José Lezama Lima
(Translated)

Masterpiece of the great poet Lezama Lima, considered to be an immense poem in prose, almost unique in the whole of literature in Spanish. The special atmosphere of this book has been compared favorably with Marcel Proust's *In Search of Lost Time.*
🔖 *Fernando Velázquez Medina, Writer and Journalist*

Paraíso Travel. *(Paradise Travel)*
Author: Jorge Franco
(Translated)

Colombian author Jorge Franco depicts in his novel *Paradise Travel* the adventures of the undocumented. Marlon, who is in love with Reina, decides to leave his home in Medellin, Colombia by following her to New York instead of going to university.
🔖 *Libbhy Romero, Brooklyn Public Library*

La parranda. *(Out on the Town)*
Author: Eduardo Blanco-Amor
(Not Translated)

A esmorga (*Out on the Town,* in Spanish *La Parranda*) was the first narrative work in Galician published by Blanco-Amor and represents one of the most unique works in all of Galician literature. It is distinguished by the richness of the

language, the sense of humor common to great part of the author's oeuvre, and a picaresque world heretofore unknown in Galician letters. The great Portuguese philosopher Rodríguez Lapa referred to it as a strange and powerful novel, whose characters appear, strong and palpable, in old Auria, speaking a language of excellent popular flavor. «It lacks nothing in order to be considered a small masterpiece.»
🔎 *Xosé Luis García Canido, Instituto Cervantes*

Los pasos perdidos. *(The Lost Steps)*
Author: Alejo Carpentier
(Translated)

One of the most important novels of Latin American literature of all times, it synthesizes the styles and themes of this distinguished author, one of the most ingenious writers in Western literature. Received an award for best foreign novel published in France in 1956.
🔎 *Fernando Velázquez Medina, Writer and Journalist*

Los peces de la amargura. *(The Fish of Bitterness)*
Author: Fernando Aramburu
(Not Translated)

Fifth novel of this already consecrated Basque author born in San Sebastián in 1959, and the first written about a typically Basque subject. From Germany, where he resides teaching Spanish language and literature as a professor of the University of Lippstandt, Aramburu has «thrust» upon us a stark, multiple-voiced novel focused on the theme of ETA violence and its social repercussions. Using a fragmented narrative as a stylistic device to perhaps avoid sentimentality, Aramburu has produced an excellent indictment against all forms of fanaticism. Before closing this brief summary, I would like to emphasize that the literary merits of this excellent author are now being recognized not only by literary critics (refer to *Fernando Aramburu, Storyteller*, written by Jose Manuel Diaz de Guereñu) but also by European publishers, as witnessed by the recent translation of *The Trumpeter of Utopia* (*El trompetista del Utopía*) into Italian, added to the translation into German of his first novel *Fires with Lemon* (*Fuegos con limón*).
🔎 *Miguel Valladares, Dartmouth College*

Pedro Páramo. *(Pedro Páramo)*
Author: Juan Rulfo
(Translated)

Pedro Páramo is one of the most important Mexican novels ever written. Besides its elaborate plot and complex characters, this text is notable for reflecting rural life in Mexico after the revolution.
🔎 *Paloma Celis Carbajal, UW-Madison*

Pequeñas resistencias: antología del nuevo cuento español.
(Light Resistance: Anthology of the New Spanish Short Story)
Author: Andrés Neuman, ed.
(Not Translated)

This anthology of thirty young Spanish short story writers, born in the 1960's and 1970's, is a strong collection based on literary quality, innovation and which contains names both canonical and truly unknown. Included is a brief biographical sketch of each other. «A short story feast.»
🔊 *Lluís Agustí, Instituto Cervantes New York*

Percusión. *(Percussion)*
Author: José Balza
(Not Translated)

A novel in which a character undertakes, with sensibility and intelligence, a voyage around the world, and becomes enlightened as to the abyss and splendors of human relations, sex, friendship, philosophy and history. *Percusión* advances like the exercising of a memory interwoven in a great game with temporality and with some of the social and individual milestones of contemporary history.
🔊 *Ernesto Pérez Zúñiga, Instituto Cervantes*

La piel fría. *(Cold Skin)*
Author: Albert Sánchez Piñol
(Translated)

In the best literary tradition of the adventure and gothic genres, (Conrad, Lovecraft, Poe), the novel *Cold Skin* recounts the adventures of a solitary lighthouse keeper in the southernmost region of the globe. On an island isolated from all civilization and battered by wind and cold, survival becomes paramount amid unknown creatures in one of the least traveled seas of the planet. An excellent work of fiction.
🔊 *Lluís Agustí, Instituto Cervantes New York*

Platero y yo. *(Platero and I)*
Author: Juan Ramón Jiménez
(Translated)

This is an enchanting book, full of grace, tenderness and nostalgia for idyllic past. Moreover, Jiménez writes with such beauty and elegance that it almost breaks your heart.
🔊 *Mark Pendleton, Branigan Library Las Cruces NM*

La plaza del diamante. *(The Time of the Doves)*
Author: Mercè Rodoreda
(Translated)

The most celebrated novel in 20th century Catalan literature and the most representative of the author's work.
🔊 *Jaume Martí Olivella, University of New Hampshire*

Plenilunio. *(Full Moon)*
Author: Rogelio Sinán
(Not Translated)

Plenilunio is the title of what may be Panamanian author Rogelio Sinán's best-known novel, written in the 1940s. Influenced by surrealist techniques, Sinán (a pseudonym adopted by Bernardo Domínguez Alba) set this interesting tale in a cabaret on the Panama Canal.
🔊 *Lluís Agustí, Instituto Cervantes New York*

Primavera con esquina rota. *(Springtime with a Broken Corner)*
Author: Mario Benedetti
(Not Translated)

An Uruguayan political prisoner longs and hopes to leave prison one day and rejoin his wife and daughter in exile. But life and love follow their course. A great storyteller whose stories absorb the reader, Mario Benedetti offers this beautiful and bittersweet novel.
🔊 *Lluís Agustí, Instituto Cervantes New York*

Los que falsificaron la firma de Dios. *(They Forged the Signature of God)*
Author: Viriato Sención
(Translated)

This is a novel of denunciation and a social, political and religious critique which takes place over three decades in a Caribbean city (Santo Domingo). The plot derives its impetus from the corruption and disorder caused by authoritarianism and modern caudillismo, focusing on characters interwoven during a period of a continuing extralegal mandate. The author incorporates magical realist passages, providing a rich touch to the narrative. This novel broke all records for sales in Dominican literary history. It was translated into English after becoming the most sold work during 1993.
🔊 *Sarah Aponte, Dominican Studies Institute, CUNY*

Rayuela. *(Hopscotch)*
Author: Julio Cortázar
(Translated)

This is an experimental, intellectual, comical and very serious novel that is known for the novelty of its design: one can read the novel straight through, or follow the author's suggested order of chapters. *Rayuela* refers to the game of hopscotch, which the latter reading resembles in format. The novel is anchored in the 1960's and 70's, and follows an Argentine's life in Paris, and his return to South America. *Rayuela* was one of the seminal «Boom» literary movement's novels.
🔊 *Lynn Shirey, Harvard College Library*

El recurso del método. *(The Resource of the Method)*
Author: Alejo Carpentier
(Translated)

Internationally acclaimed writer Alejo Carpentier gives us this telling of the story of a dictator of an unnamed country in Latin America (could be Cuba, Dominican Republic, Paraguay) and how he deals with conspiracies, a student uprising engineered by the communists, and denies the subjugated peasantry of even their humble status in his society.
🔊 *Alina San Juan, Trade Comission of Spain*

La Regenta. *(La Regenta)*
Author: Leopoldo Alas «Clarín»
(Translated)

One of the great novels of the 19th century which vividly transports us to the world of the small city, prisoner of religious conditioning and social class barriers. *La Regenta* is one of the most enchanting female characters in Spanish literature, richly detailed and full of psychological subtlety, and proceeding from a world and time when feminine passion dare not speak its name.
🔊 *Elvira Lindo, Writer and Journalist*

La reina del sur. *(The Queen of the South)*
Author: Arturo Pérez-Reverte
(Translated)

Elected to the Spanish Royal Academy in 2002, Arturo Pérez-Reverte is a novelist and long time career journalist. In *The Queen of the South*, the author centers his sixth novel in the frightening and fascinating world of drug trafficking throughout Mexico, southern Spain and Morocco. The story portrays the life of a young Mexican, Teresa Mendoza, whose boyfriend, a drug-runner and pilot named Raimundo Davila Parra is killed when his plane is shot down by a couple of hit men.
🔊 *Libbhy Romero, Brooklyn Public Library*

El reino de este mundo. *(The Kingdom of this World)*
Author: Alejo Carpentier
(Translated)

The Kingdom of this World is one of those books which capture and amaze you in a real and marvelous world which will not let you be until you have read each and every one of its pages.
🔻 *Paloma Celis Carbajal, UW-Madison*

Réquiem por un campesino español. *(Requiem for a Spanish Peasant)*
Author: Ramón J. Sender
(Translated)

In Aragon, Mosén Millán, a village priest, prepares to officiate a mass for the soul of Paco el Molinero, a village youth executed in the first days of the Civil War because of his progressive ideas. The priest had baptized the young man, had educated him, and had even chosen him to be his altar boy. When Paco is forced to go into hiding, after the political events which precipitated the war, Mosén Millán, wishing to help the young man, urges him to give himself up. Paco is sentenced to the firing squad, and the priest will be obliged to hear his confession before the execution.
🔻 *Lluís Agustí, Instituto Cervantes New York*

Respiración artificial. *(Artificial Respiration)*
Author: Ricardo Piglia
(Translated)

In the novel *Respiración artificial* a group of friends discuss Argentine literature and writers. It's a wonder for two reasons: on the one hand, it vindicates the coffeehouse model, rather than the academy, as the natural forum to discuss those subjects, and on the other, it criticizes officially consecrated high priests with great wisdom and humor.
🔻 *Silvia Gil de Cwilich, Artist and Reader*

Reunión de cuentos. *(Collected Short Stories)*
Author: Jesús Gardea
(Not Translated)

The recently late Mexican writer Jesús Gardea (1939-2000) stands out in the panorama of Mexican letters by his idiosyncratic use of the Spanish language, by means of which he creates a self-contained universe developed in the course of several novels. Following the trail blazed by Guimaraes Rosa and Lezama Lima, Gardea, in the short stories collected in this volume, concentrates the essential traits of the narrator's craft, striking a balance between the most rigorous control of language and the greatest of imaginative liberties.
🔻 *Gaspar Orozco, Mexican Poet and Diplomat*

Los ríos profundos. *(Deep Rivers)*
Author: José María Arguedas
(Translated)

The beauty and the violence which the young narrator encounters in his travels throughout the Andes are portrayed with tenderness and deep understanding in this autobiographical novel.
🔍 *Richard Heyer, Instituto Cervantes New York*

Los rojos de ultramar. *(Overseas Reds)*
Author: Jordi Soler
(Not Translated)

In this cross of memoir, historical document and novel, Mexican writer Jordi Soler, grandson of Republican Spaniards, tells the story of his grandfather Arcadi's arrival in the country and of the founding of a community of exiled Catalans in the middle of the Veracruzan forest. The objective of the community is not just survival as individuals or as a group, more than mere survival, what moves the group is the idea of return.
🔍 *Lluís Agustí, Instituto Cervantes New York*

Rosario Tijeras. *(Rosario Tijeras: A Novel)*
Author: Jorge Franco
(Translated)

Story told from the point of view of a young man about his love for an assassin in Medellin, Colombia. Rosario loves Emilio but confides in Pacero. The latter recounts the friendship of the threesome, while Rosario lies dying in a hospital bed after being shot.
🔍 *Scott Van Jacob, University of Notre Dame*

Rosas de papel. *(Paper Roses)*
Author: Olga Nolla
(Not Translated)

Olga Nolla transports us to Puerto Rico in the 1930's, presenting the hybrid nature of Puerto Rican reality, but this time through the history of one of its privileged families.
🔍 *Sabrina Abreu, Instituto Cervantes New York*

El rufián moldavo. *(The Moldavian Ruffian)*
Author: Edgardo Cozarinsky
(Not Translated)

During the first half of 20th century, Argentina harbored a Jewish criminal organization called Zwi Migdal. This mafia style organization was formed by Jewish procurers who recruited young Jewish women from Russia, Galicia, and other parts of Eastern Europe to be prostitutes throughout Argentina. The Jewish community rejected outright, in life and in death, both the members of Zwi Migdal and their victims. An Argentine residing in Paris, and descendant of artists in Buenos Aires Yiddish theater of that time, repeats and closes a family circle without knowing it. A portentous narrative from the Argentine filmmaker and writer Edgardo Cozarinsky, and a stroke of luck for those who not yet read the novel.

🔹 *Lluís Agustí, Instituto Cervantes New York*

San Manuel Bueno Mártir. *(Saint Manuel Bueno, Martyr)*
Author: Miguel de Unamuno
(Not Translated)

For those who believe, for those who want to believe and for those who no longer belive, Unamuno's novel will challenge all and force them to rethink their faith.

🔹 *Adan Griego, Stanford University Libraries*

Semblanzas del corazón. *(Sketches of the Heart)*
Author: José Rafael Lantigua
(Not Translated)

Semblanzas inscribes past events and experiences into the present collective memory, evoking in nostalgic episodes of what the Dominican town of Moca represented in the past. Lantigua pays homage to the many men and women who contributed to the social and human formation of the mocano of today.

🔹 *Nashieli Marcano, University of Akron*

El señor Presidente. *(The President)*
Author: Miguel Ángel Asturias
(Translated)

Guatemalan writer Miguel Ángel Asturias, winner of the Nobel Prize in Literature, is the author of *El señor Presidente*, an outstanding novel about a Latin American tyrant. Sadly, this literary tradition has been explored by Spanish-language authors because the character recurs so often. The best-known works in this genre are *Yo, el Supremo*, by Augusto Roa Bastos, *El recurso del método*, by Alejo Carpentier, and more recently *La Fiesta del Chivo*, by Mario Vargas Llosa. This book by Miguel Ángel Asturias—based on the figure of the Guatemalan dictator Manuel Estrada Cabrera—is particularly notable because it is one of the first works in this area, and it has a strength and vigor that remain fresh today.

🔹 *Lluís Agustí, Instituto Cervantes New York*

Si te dicen que caí. *(The Fallen)*
Author: Juan Marsé
(Translated)

One of the fundamental works of modern fiction written in Spain, which placed the Spanish novel in the top echelons of 20th century prose in any language, after the breakdown brought on by the Civil War. The perfect marriage between bold language and likable characters, born in the alleyways produced by the war, make this an indispensable novel in the history of our literature.
🔖 *Ernesto Pérez Zúñiga, Instituto Cervantes*

El siglo de las luces. *(A Century of Lights)*
Author: Alejo Carpentier
(Translated)

Through Victor Hughes we follow the impact of the French Revolution in the Antilles, where the inhabitants dream of freedom while the guillotine casts its deadly shadow. A novel that can be identified as a true representative of magic realism, and which gives the reader a comprehensive portrait of the atmosphere surrounding the Age of Enlightment.
🔖 *Alina San Juan, Trade Comission of Spain*

Sin noticias de Gurb. *(No News from Gurb)*
Author: Eduardo Mendoza
(Not Translated)

This is one of the most fun books that I've read and Eduardo Mendoza is a master of the written word. I also like his other books.
🔖 *María José Durán Silva, G.W.: Carver Middle School*

Sin ti no soy yo. *(Without You, I Am not Myself)*
Author: Lourdes Vázquez
(Not Translated)

It is a story of pleasures and tragedies with «espiritismo» and «santería» as backdrop, set in mid-20th century Puerto Rico. The characters, bound by family ties, are taken into a whirlpool of emotions and passions, which as a result, constructs their collective reality.
🔖 *Nashieli Marcano, University of Akron*

Soldados. *(Soldiers)*
Author: Francisco González Ledesma
(Not Translated)

While some of his works were censored in Spain during the Franco period, Spanish journalist and novelist Francisco González Ledesma was financially forced to produce a Western novella per week under the pseudonym of Silver Kane. From the journalist's trade, which requires the constant and forced exercise of telling stories, there emerged an authentic writer, whose style is clear, precise, relevant and highly evocative. Moreover, González Ledesma is faithful to his people and to his humble origins. *Soldados* is the story of the three old men from those old neighborhoods, who at the end of their lives and for different reasons —curiosity, vengeance or desperation— start off together on a search.
🔊 *Lluís Agustí, Instituto Cervantes New York*

Soldados de Salamina. *(Soldiers of Salamis)*
Author: Javier Cercas
(Translated)

Rafael Sánchez Mazas was a well-known Spanish Falangist writer and politician who was captured by the Republican government during the Civil War. During the final withdrawal of the army to the French border, he was taken before a firing squad and seemed certain to die. The research undertaken by an academic to clarify the elements of this story, becomes a search to discover the identity of the soldier who saved Sánchez Mazas from certain death, and more importantly, to discover his purpose for doing so. An extraordinary work about heroism, love, the passage of time and the recovery of the memories of the disappeared.
🔊 *Lluís Agustí, Instituto Cervantes New York*

Solitud. *(Solitude: A Novel)*
Author: Víctor Català
(Translated)

The best novel inspired by Catalan Modernism, and an authentic precursor of the women's literature (Víctor Català, pseud. of Caterina Albert) which would play such an important role in the Catalan literary world.
🔊 *Jaume Martí Olivella, University of New Hampshire*

Sólo cenizas hallarás (bolero). *(You'll Only Find Ashes (Bolero))*
Author: Pedro Vergés
(Not Translated)

This novel reflects Dominican society in the years following the death of dictator Rafael Trujillo (1961-1962). The characters' lives mirror the great economic and socio-cultural changes the country was undergoing at that time. The phenomenon of immigration to the United States is analyzed through the characters of Freddy and Yolanda. Freddy represents the young Dominican who sees immigration as the solution to all his financial troubles. Yolanda represents the young woman without much motivation who returns to live in Santo Domingo (the capital of the Dominican Republic) and who faces the problems of adaptation and acclimatization. Verges presents us with a social novel of daily life in simple language, the language of the barrio, of a people.
Sarah Aponte, Dominican Studies Institute. CUNY

La sombra del viento. *(The Shadow of the Wind)*
Author: Carlos Ruiz Zafón
(Translated)

A wonderful gothic novel involving a secret library and illicit loves in post-Civil War Barcelona.
Lynn Shirey, Harvard College Library

Son de mar. *(Song of the Sea)*
Author: Manuel Vicent
(Not Translated)

This is a beautiful novel written with a magnificent prose yet easy to read. Manuel Vicent won with this book the Alfaguara prize in 1999.
Alvaro Sanabria, San Francisco Public Library

La sonrisa etrusca. *(The Etruscan Smile)*
Author: José Luis Sampedro
(Not Translated)

At the end of his life, sick and lonely, an old Italian fighter spends his last days in the company of his daughter and grandson in a Northern Italian city. A beautiful work about the meaning of life, memories, friendship and love.
Lluís Agustí, Instituto Cervantes New York

Spiks. *(Spiks; stories)*
Author: Pedro Juan Soto
(Translated)

Soto presents a collection of short stories written in the 1950's and 1960's, in which he describes the changing role of the Puerto Rican women in the urban environment.
🔊 *Nashieli Marcano, University of Akron*

Sueños y discursos. *(Dreams and Discourses)*
Author: Francisco de Quevedo
(Translated)

The *Sueños* consist of five visions of hell, visited by the author in his dreams. He encounters people of various social classes and professions being punished for their sins and lampoons them hasrshly with his mordant wit. This work is both the bitterest and most amusing satire of the Golden Age.
🔊 *Eduardo de Lamadrid, Trans-Lingual Communications Inc.*

El Sur; seguido de Bene. *(The South; and, Bene)*
Author: Adelaida García Morales
(Translated)

A novel about a young Spanish woman's memories of her childhood in Sevilla, which prove to be erroneous.
🔊 *Lynn Shirey, Harvard College Library*

Tengo miedo torero. *(My Tender Matador)*
Author: Pedro Lemebel
(Translated)

Lemebel, the «enfant terrible» of current Chilean writing, had been writing on the «margins» during the Pinochet dictatorship. His text captures with much wit that tragic time for his country with the voice of some one who has endured that tragedy for not conforming to the norm. When asked once, if he wanted to play with dolls as a child, he noted, «I wanted to be the doll!» That's the beauty of Lemebel's narrative, recently translated into English as *My Tender Matador*.
🔊 *Adan Griego, Stanford University Libraries*

Terrazo. *(Terrazo)*
Author: Abelardo Díaz Alfaro
(Not Translated)

This highly acclaimed short-story collection by Díaz Alfaro encompasses the struggle of the islanders in rural Puerto Rico, engaging in a lyrical language when describing the countryside landscape.
🔍 *Nashieli Marcano, University of Akron*

Tesis de un homicidio. *(Thesis of a Murder)*
Author: Diego Paszkowski
(Not Translated)

Paul, the aristocratic son of an Argentine diplomat in France, travels to Buenos Aires to take a course in Criminal Law. There we encounter Paul's professor, who witnesses a crime right in front of the office of the School of Law. He suspects one of his students and becomes obsessed with finding him. Concomitantly, Paul becomes obsessed with an actress, for whom he searches in all women. A cinematographic novel and impossible to put down.
🔍 *Martha Berman, Professor of Language and Literature*

El testigo. *(The Witness)*
Author: Juan Villoro
(Not Translated)

The first classic novel to appear in Mexico after the political changes, *The Witness* offers the reader a fully realized panorama of a country in which the vestiges and phantoms of the past coexist daily with the wounds of a schizophrenic and convulsive present. Under a climate which has reached a boiling point, Juan Villoro (1956) relates in a precise and intelligent style the odyssey of a Mexican professor who returns to his native land after a long absence. As in the Homeric epic, he discovers that the return to Ithaca is impossible.
🔍 *Bruno Hernández Piché, Mexican Writer and Diplomat*

Tirant lo Blanc. *(Tirant lo Blanc)*
Author: Joanot Martorell
(Translated)

The fundamental novel of medieval Catalan literature and the first modern novel in the critical consideration of Mario Vargas Llosa.
🔍 *Jaume Martí Olivella, University of New Hampshire*

Travesuras de la niña mala. *(The Bad Girl's Pranks)*
Author: Mario Vargas Llosa
(Not Translated)

A new masterpiece from one of the best contemporary writers in Spanish. Creatively and carefully structured, this work is a reflection on love from a singular point of view, which blends fiction and reality in an impeccable manner.
 Julio Rivas, Reader

El tren pasa primero. *(The Train Goes By First)*
Author: Elena Poniatowska
(Not Translated)

Poniatowska should be on an essential list. She is well-known for her journalism and political commentary in Mexico. This is a novel about the railroad movement in Mexico acclaimed at the Guadalajara Book Fair.
 Millie Torrance, Sacramento Public Library

Tres tristes tigres. *(Three Trapped Tigers)*
Author: Guillermo Cabrera Infante
(Translated)

An unclassifiable book, a conjunction of journalistic, literary and cinematographic techniques, it constitutes a unique case in Hispanic literature. An immense play on words elevated to the category of great literature which proved extremely influential in Latin America.
 Fernando Velázquez Medina, Writer and Journalist

Trilogía sucia de La Habana. *(Dirty Havana Trilogy)*
Author: Pedro Juan Gutiérrez
(Translated)

Written in strong and aggressive language, which is almost a kick in the chest to the reader, this is a collection of three stories, which resemble, by their unity of style and characterization, an experimental novel. A best seller which is, above all, good literature.
 Fernando Velázquez Medina, Writer and Journalist

El turno de Anacle: cuentos. *(Anacle's Turn: Stories)*
Author: Galo Galarza
(Not Translated)

Author of brief yet polished narratives, Ecuadorian writer Galo Galarza offers us a gallery of extraordinary characters in this unforgettable anthology of stories.
🔍 *Lluís Agustí, Instituto Cervantes New York*

Tuyo es el reino. *(Thine is the Kingdom)*
Author: Abilio Estévez
(Translated)

Acclaimed by European critics, *The New York Times* and readers, Abilio Estévez's first novel won the Prize for the best foreign novel published in France in 2000. A work that surely would have been praised by Virgilio Piñera, mentor and teacher of Abilio Estévez.
🔍 *Fernando Velázquez Medina, Writer and Journalist*

La última escala del Tramp Steamer.
(Last Port of Call for the Tramp Steamer)
Author: Álvaro Mutis
(Not Translated)

The voyages of the Alción, a dilapidated freighter, in search of occasional cargoes parallels, in imagery and sense, the shipwreck of the love of its Captain, the Basque Jon Iturri, for the Lebanese girl Warda Bashur, younger sister of the ship's owner. The search for one more port before the tramp steamer gives out corresponds to Jon's obstinate desire for Warda, to a love condemned to disaster beforehand, to a pair of lovers separated by an unbridgeable gulf.
🔍 *Lluís Agustí, Instituto Cervantes New York*

La última noche de Dostoievski. *(Dostoevsky's Last Night)*
Author: Cristina Peri Rossi
(Translated)

A player narrates a life of regrets, as he confronts his obsession with the help of a psychologist.
🔍 *Scott Van Jacob, University of Notre Dame*

El último Catón. *(The Last Cato: A Novel)*
Author: Matilde Asensi
(Translated)

This is a perfect book for readers who have enjoyed the novels of Dan Brown and Umberto Eco. However, this book was published before *The Da Vinci Code* and perhaps Dan Brown is in the debt of this marvelous author.
🔖 *Gabriel Partlow, Pima County Public Library*

La verdad sospechosa. *(The Suspect Truth)*
Author: Juan Ruiz de Alarcón
(Translated)

The bow-legged and hunchbacked Ruiz de Alarcón was the 17th century's greatest writer of thesis plays and had a great influence on Corneille, Molière and Goldoni. His forte was the development of character types that represent vices and illustrate moral truths. *La verdad sospechosa* inveighs against the vice of lying, while combining entertainment with ethical teaching. Alarcón was the most modern of his contemporaries and the greatest moralist of the Spanish classical theater.
🔖 *Eduardo de Lamadrid, Trans-Lingual Communications Inc.*

La vida del Buscón. *(The Life of a Swindler)*
Author: Francisco de Quevedo
(Translated)

This brilliant and cynical novel, supposedly containing many autobiographical episodes, and set in a boarding house in Salamanca peopled by unsavory characters, is one of the wittiest books ever written in Spanish, so packed with conceits and double meanings that it is all but impossible to translate.
🔖 *Eduardo de Lamadrid, Trans-Lingual Communications Inc.*

La vida exagerada de Martín Romaña.
(The Exaggerated Life of Martín Romaña)
Author: Alfredo Bryce Echenique
(Not Translated)

Pinnacle of what some critics have called the new sentimental novel, this work, informed in part by certain topoi of the picaresque novel, presents one of the most likeable and delicious characters in Spanish 20th century literature. Martin Romaña exemplifies a new form of masculinity, which involves tenderness, the profusion of sentiment, verbal play and an uncontainable and fascinating sense of humor.
🔖 *Ernesto Pérez Zúñiga, Instituto Cervantes*

La vida perra de Juanita Narboni.
(The Unbearable Life of Juanita Narboni)
Author: Ángel Vázquez
(Not Translated)

There was a time during the 20th century in Spain when certain monarchs, dictators, politicians and military officers dreamt of once again gilding coats of arms, some businessmen saw an opportunity, and many Spaniards gave their blood. After the loss of the empire in 1898, the sad 20th century campaigns in Morocco were an attempt to reorganize the dream in African land. After the army came the colonizers in search of hope. A considerable number of Spaniards settled in Tetouan, Larache or Tangier, international city occupied by Franco during the World War II, in this way creating a peculiar culture, apparently Spanish but sharing other indigenous and colonial traits. With the independence of Morocco in 1956 comes the diaspora, the fracture of the dream to which some cling, like Juanita Narboni. The essential novel about Tangier.

 Lluís Agustí, Instituto Cervantes New York

El viento de la luna. *(The Moon Wind)*
Author: Antonio Muñoz Molina
(Not Translated)

The Moon Wind recounts the life of a provincial adolescent in Francoist Spain during a week of the month of July 1969. While man is walking on the moon, the adolescent lives in a world anchored in the earth. In this constricted world, he discovers the reality of life, society, and sex, the weight of his being and of those who surround him, loyalty and his father's worth. Magisterially narrated by one of the best contemporary Spanish writers.

Lluís Agustí, Instituto Cervantes New York

Vírgenes y mártires. *(Virgins and Martyrs)*
Author: Ana Lydia Vega
(Not Translated)

In this innovative collection containing six of her stories and six written by Carmen Lugo Filippi, the authors highlight various social aspects of Puerto Rican society of the 1970's, seen through the colonial lens.

Nashieli Marcano, University of Akron

La vorágine. *(The Vortex)*
Author: José Eustaquio Rivera
(Translated)

La vorágine is one of the most important and interesting works in Colombian literature, and indeed of Latin American literature as a whole during the first half of the 20th century. The novel's denunciation of the working conditions of Colombian rubber tappers in the jungle is its starting point but not its final result. *La vorágine* has served as an inspiration and a reinterpretation for an entire generation of Spanish American novelists.
Lluís Agustí, Instituto Cervantes New York

El vuelo de la reina. *(Flight of the Queen)*
Author: Tomás Eloy Martínez
(Not Translated)

An amazing book about the obsession that well known publisher Camargo has for a young reporter Remis. The political events of Argentina are intertwined in this intriguing story also about power and control. I was intrigued and scared by Camargo and his seemingly dual personality. His sexual voyeurism was both fascinating and revolting. This book won the Premio Alfaguara in 2002.
Millie Torrance, Sacramento Public Library

Yo el supremo. *(I, the Supreme)*
Author: Augusto Roa Bastos
(Translated)

Paraguayan novelist and poet, Augusto Antonio Roa Bastos, who received the Cervantes Prize in letters in 1989, recounts in this modern Latin American classic and masterpiece, the imagined life of the last royal governor voted dictator, Gaspar Rodríguez de Francia while covering more than 100 years of Paraguayan history.
Libbhy Romero, Brooklyn Public Library

Yo me perdono. *(I Absolve Myself)*
Author: Fietta Jarque
(Not Translated)

The cultural and religious shock experienced by colonial Peru is manifested in the mestizo art of the Cuzco school and in the lives of four men: a young painter, an Indian, a priest, and a businessman who unite to make the church of Andahuaylillas a center of religious power.
Richard Heyer, Instituto Cervantes New York

Zorro. *(Zorro)*
Author: Isabel Allende
(Translated)

This is my second favorite book of Allende's. I enjoyed the new twist and the telling of this legend from the point of view of a woman —a surprise until the end.
📣 *Millie Torrance, Sacramento Public Library*

POETRY
DRAMA

5 metros de poemas. *(Five Meters of poems)*
Author: Carlos Oquendo de Amat
(Not Translated)

«Open this book as if you were peeling a fruit». That's the opening sentence of this genial work originally published in 1927. Evincing some influence from the cinema and surrealism, the book's very original imagery and style are displayed in the five meters of its titile.
🔊 *Richard Heyer, Instituto Cervantes New York*

Al sur de mi garganta. *(South of My Throat)*
Author: Carilda Oliver Labra
(Not Translated)

Sensual and erotic poetry, it defined an era of women's poetry, both in Cuba and abroad. It had great impact in the intellectual world of the last half century, is still relevant today, and is the subject of much admiration and discussion in Cuba.
🔊 *Fernando Velázquez Medina, Writer and Journalist*

Altazor o el viaje en paracaídas.
(Altazor, or a Voyage in a Parachute: Poem in VII Cantos)
Author: Vicente Huidobro
(Translated)

I love Huidobro's character: the ferocity, optimism and impertinence of *Non serviam*. It is said that Huidobro entered Berlin with the Russians just to steal Hitler's telephone. *Altazor* is a delectable and ingenious book, full of playful metaphors, almost like a toy train set or a city in miniature.
🔊 *Blanca Riestra, Instituto Cervantes Albuquerque*

Anatomía de la palabra. *(Anatomy of the Word)*
Author: José Ángel Valente
(Not Translated)

From inception, José Ángel Valente's poetry unleashes the struggle to decipher the primal myth of the primeval word, capable in and of itself of harboring confusion and chaos. But in parallel emerge the signifiers of History which take control of the diachronic and sedimentary condition of language. «In the balance», wrote José Miguel Ullán, «two worlds: poetry which creates truth, truth which creates poetry.»
🔊 *Xosé Luis García Canido, Instituto Cervantes*

Anatomía del deseo. *(Anatomy of Desire)*
Author: Ricardo Cobián Figeroux
(Not Translated)

In this dialogic and polyphonic piece, the author presents an eloquent experience of the pleasures of poetry. The discursive and metaphoric space of the poet-spectator, acquires an intimate and performative character, defining «desire» as the ultimate point of no return.
🐟 *Nashieli Marcano, University of Akron*

Animal de fondo. *(Animal of the Deep)*
Author: Juan Ramón Jiménez
(Not Translated)

«I am an animal of the deep», he writes, and somewhere else, «Desiring and desired God». The later Jiménez is an example of faith in the word, of a vital and heterodox mysticism, of the purity of poetry freed from all limitations.
🐟 *Blanca Riestra, Instituto Cervantes Albuquerque*

Antología de la poesía boliviana: ordenar la danza.
(Anthology of Bolivian Poetry: Organizing the Dance)
Author: Mónica Velásquez Guzmán, ed.
(Not Translated)

A recent, up-to-date anthology of 20th-century Bolivian poetry. Presented in chronological order, it opens with Ricardo Jaimes Freyre, one of Bolivia's most famous poets, and also includes works by such well-known poets as Franz Tamayo, Gregorio Reynolds, Óscar Cerruto and Eduardo Mitre. The book covers a total of 49 poets in all.
🐟 *Lluís Agustí, Instituto Cervantes New York*

Antología del grupo poético de 1927.
(Anthology of the Poetic Generation of 1927)
Author: Vicente Gaos, ed.
(Not Translated)

Although there are critics who cast doubt on the reality of literary generations or groupings, the use of such classifications has enjoyed some success in the presentation of the literary history of a language, and more specifically, of a country. If we refer to the generation of Spanish writers, many of them poets, from the interwar period, the so called Generation of 1927, then undoubtedly that grouping has become an icon, a landmark. Pedro Salinas, Federico García Lorca, Vicente Aleixandre, Jorge Guillén, Gerardo Diego, Rafael Alberti, Emilio Prados, Dámaso Alonso, Luis Cernuda, and Manuel Altolaguirre represent the best of 20th century Spanish poetry.

Lluís Agustí, Instituto Cervantes New York

Antología personal. *(Personal Anthology)*
Author: José Agustín Goytisolo
(Not Translated)

The Goytisolos, three brothers and writers: José Agustín, poet and translator, Juan and Luis, both storytellers. Jose Agustín Goytisolo, the eldest of the three, belongs to the poetic generation of 1950, committed to the resistance against Francoism, and like many of the bohemian group, a lover of personal freedom and a great vitalist, sometimes to excess. As Carlos Barral said when referring to them all, «we drank too much.» José Agustín Goytisolo's poetry gives expression to that personal option and breaks with all forms of academism, in real and honest verse that makes no concessions, poetry that emanate from the vital impulse itself.

Lluís Agustí, Instituto Cervantes New York

Antología poética. *(Tugs in the Fog: Selected Poems)*
Author: Joan Margarit
(Translated)

A dazzling Catalan poet, in a bilingual edition (the translation into Spanish is the author's own).

José María Conget, Writer

Antología poética. *(Anthology of Poetry)*
Author: Jorge Enrique Adoum
(Not Translated)

There are epic poets who write in verse and compose anthems in praise of the nation's triumphs, but the Ecuadorean poet Jorge Enrique Adoum is surely not one of them. Beginning with his first book, *Ecuador amargo*, *(Bitter Equador)* Adoum has put together a body of work in which he examines and rewrites the history of his country, people and continent.

Lluís Agustí, Instituto Cervantes New York

Antología poética. *(Selected Verses)*
Author: Federico García Lorca
(Translated)

A classic. *Millie Torrance, Sacramento Public Library*

Antología poética. *(Anthology of Poetry)*
Author: Josefina Pla
(Not Translated)

Josefina Pla, Spanish by birth and Paraguayan by choice, left numerous works ranging from poetry and short stories to theater. She is a key figure in understanding 20th-century Paraguayan culture and the way it has developed, especially poetry. Her poems are characterized by their intimate and accessible tone with references to current events, particularly the role and status of women.
 Lluís Agustí, Instituto Cervantes New York

Antología poética.
(Roads Dreamed Clear Afternoons: An Anthology of the Poetry of Antonio Machado)
Author: Antonio Machado
(Translated)

Indispensable. *Millie Torrance, Sacramento Public Library*

El arpa imaginaria. *(The Imaginary Harp)*
Author: Edwin Reyes
(Not Translated)

Inspired by a great uncle who «sang verses accompanying himself on an imaginary instrument,» this collection of poems demonstrates the quality of a poet fully in touch with his people. Edwin Reyes is one of the most original voices in Puerto Rican poetry.
 Sabrina Abreu, Instituto Cervantes New York

Azul. *(Stories and Poems)*
Author: Rubén Darío
(Translated)

This book reflects some of the most significant periods of the greatest Nicaraguan poet who became very significant to future generations of Latin American poets.
 Alvaro Sanabria, San Francisco Public Library

El azul de la tierra. *(The Blue Earth)*
Author: Eugenio Montejo
(Not Translated)

This Venezuelan poet is one of the greatest lyricists in the Spanish language, but remains relatively unknown in Spain.
🔹 *José María Conget, Writer*

Azul; España contemporánea; Cantos de vida y esperanza.
(Stories and Poems)
Author: Rubén Darío
(Translated)

Darío is probably the most important Nicaraguan poet and his work is beautiful and compact. He had a great influence on the generation which followed.
🔹 *Millie Torrance, Sacramento Public Library*

Bodas de sangre. *(Blood Wedding)*
Author: Federico García Lorca
(Translated)

Based on a true story, *Blood Wedding* is one of the most powerful, inventive and recognized plays written in modern Spanish literature.
🔹 *Alvaro Sanabria, San Francisco Public Library*

El bosque transparente (poesía, 1971-1981)
(The Transparent Forest (Poetry, 1971-1981))
Author: Ángel Crespo
(Not Translated)

The Manchegan Ángel Crespo, besides being a poet, is an excellent essayist, critic and translator. *The Transparent Forest* collects the majority of his poetical works, namely the five books he wrote while living outside of Spain during tenures as a professor at universities in Puerto Rico, Leiden, Venice, and Washington.
🔹 *Lluís Agustí, Cervantes Institute, New York*

El burlador de Sevilla. *(The Trickster of Seville)*
Author: Tirso de Molina
(Translated)

Pseudonym of Gabriel Téllez, a Mercederian friar, Tirso de Molina created the first Don Juan drama in world literature. Tirso's hero, Don Juan Tenorio became the inpiration for Moliere, Mozart, Byron and Zorrilla, to cite only the most famous treatments of the theme. Don Juan Tenorio, in Tirso's version, is a titanic character whose reckless defiance of the moral code reaches a level of superhuman courage, which to some extent, redeems his libertinism.
🔹 *Eduardo de Lamadrid, Trans-Lingual Communications Inc.*

La caja negra. *(The Black Box)*
Author: Juan Carlos Quintero
(Not Translated)

This rich and hermetic book of poems contains a collection of verses that brings together multiple tones and cultural traditions, in a very Caribbean style.
Nashieli Marcano, University of Akron

Campos de Castilla. *(The Landscape of Castile)*
Author: Antonio Machado
(Translated)

The Sevillian poet Antonio Machado is one of the greatest Spanish poets of all times, while at the same time being the most popular poet in the peninsula. His verse, simple in appearance, comprehensible and familiar, has the power to reach the reader in a sincere and emotional way. He takes as his theme an almost anthropological approach to the country's way of life and its people, exemplified in sad image of the two Spains. A life marked by personal (the death of his wife) and social misfortunes (the Civil War), surfaces in his verse, endowing them with honesty and experience. *The Landscape of Castile*, his third published work, owes its title to the period when he lived in Soria, where he was a professor.
Lluís Agustí, Instituto Cervantes New York

Cancionero y romancero de ausencias.
(The Selected Poems of Miguel Hernández)
Author: Miguel Hernández
(Translated)

In 1930's Spain, Miguel Hernández was a poet of the people and for the people. His determined conduct during the Civil War led to his death in prison in 1942. During the time he was imprisoned, he wrote this beautiful and tragic collection of poems, full of authentic and profound imagery.
Lluís Agustí, Instituto Cervantes New York

Cantar de Mío Cid. *(Poem of the Cid)*
Author: Anonymous
(Translated)

The great medieval Spanish epic, composed by an unknown Castilian juglar (minstrel) in about 1140, but which is preserved in a single copy of 1307 transcribed by one Per Abbat, of whom nothing is known. The reconstructed epic known as the *Cantar de Mío Cid* (*Song of My Cid*) is based on other historical materials and is of much later date. The plot of the *Poem of the Cid* is divided into three parts: the banishment of Rodrigo Díaz (El Cid) by his sovereign; the

Cid's victory over the Moors at Valencia, reconciliation with the king, and marriage of his daughters into royalty; and the desertion and cruel treatment of his daughters and trial by combat of the sons-in-law, resulting in the vindication of the Cid's honor. The oldest monument of Castilian literature, the Poem of the Cid is admirable for its realism, its comparative historical fidelity, its fusion of various themes into a unified whole, and as the first and best example of the Spanish «cantar de gesta».

🔖 *Eduardo de Lamadrid, Trans-Lingual Communications Inc.*

Cantigas de Santa María. *(Canticles for Holy Mary)*
Author: Alfonso X el Sabio
(Translated)

This collection of 420 songs, set to music and gloryfing the miracles performed by the Virgin Mary, was composed by a 13th century king, known as the Wise or the Sage, who was the greatest of all medieval patrons of letters, an encyclopedic scholar and a poet in his own right. Of great power and musicality, the songs were written in Galician, the literary language of the age. Alfonso the Wise also exercised great influence on the development of Castilian prose with works on the law, history and astronomy.

🔖 *Eduardo de Lamadrid, Trans-Lingual Communications Inc.*

Cantos de vida y esperanza. *(Songs of Life and Hope)*
Author: Rubén Darío
(Translated)

This work by the great Nicaraguan poet sets forth exotic themes as well as themes about the poet's «search for his own self». Rubén Darío is considered by many critics to be one of the most influential modernist poets from Latin America. These poems touch upon exotic themes and the poet's quest for spiritual fulfilment.

🔖 *Ismael Alicea, The New York Public Library*

La casa de Bernarda Alba. *(The House of Bernarda Alba)*
Author: Federico García Lorca
(Translated)

Considered to be Lorca's highest dramatic achievement, besides being one of the most well-known and dramatized works of the Spanish theater. The subtitle of the play is *Drama of Women in the Villages of Spain*. It focuses on the life of an Andalusian family in which the protagonist exercises a cruel tyranny over her five daughters. This drama explores the themes of repression, passion and nonconformity in a rural feminine world. It is worth noting the apparent simplicity of the work counterpoised against its enormous thematic complexity.

🔖 *Paloma Celis Carbajal, UW-Madison*

El castillo interior o las moradas. *(The Interior Castle or the Chambers)*
Author: Santa Teresa de Jesús
(Translated)

Santa Teresa de Jesús represents the humanization of mysticism. In her greatest mystical work, she narrates the ascent of her soul through the seven chambers of the mystic castle to complete union with God. Her basic message is the extinction of self and submergence into the Divine Essence. Yet her style is conversational and full of native humor and pungency. Her many achievements are related in her *Libro de las fundaciones* and her inner life is revealed in her introspective autobiography, *Libro de su vida.*
🔖 *Eduardo de Lamadrid, Trans-Lingual Communications Inc.*

La Celestina. *(The Celestina: A Novel in Dialogue)*
Author: Fernando de Rojas
(Translated)

This dramatized novel is considered by critics second only to Don Quixote in intrinsic greatness and literary influence. The plot deals with the love of Calisto for Melibea, whose initial indifference prompts him to engage the services of a go-between, who deviously persuades the girl to respond to her lover's suit. It ends tragically with the death of both lovers. The greatness of the novel lies in its realistic delineation of character. The crone, Celestina, a panderess of titanic cunning, is depicted as evil incarnate. Other characters such as the picaresque servants, the prostitutes, the braggart soldiers etc. present a vivid pictue of life among the common people of early 16th century Spain. Even Calisto, with his flowery diction and his abject adoration, is a faithful portrayal of the Petrarcan lover of the day.
🔖 *Eduardo de Lamadrid, Trans-Lingual Communications Inc.*

Cien sonetos de amor. *(One Hundred Love Sonnets)*
Author: Pablo Neruda
(Translated)

This work is very popular as well as being beautiful.
🔖 *Millie Torrance, Sacramento Public Library*

El cristal. *(Glass)*
Author: Jorge Fernández Granados
(Not Translated)

One of the most profound voices in current Mexican poetry belongs to Jorge Fernández Granados. *El cristal* (Mexico City, 1995) is a collection of 54 prose poems, genre in which Fernández has reached the fullness of maturity in a major key. Translucent machines, vehicles for profound poetic explorations, the texts which comprise this book are united by a silent visionary will and an expressive impulse which vacillates between presence and absence.

🔖 *Gaspar Orozco, Mexican Poet and Diplomat*

El decir y el vértigo: panorama de la poesía hispanoamericana reciente (1963-1979). *(Expression and Vertigo: Overview of Contemporary Hispanic-American Poetry, 1963-1979)*
Author: Rocío Cerón, Julián Herbert, and León Plascencia Ñol
(Not Translated)

The anthologists, active poets with important works of their own and experienced editors, have taken on the arduous task of offering an overview of Hispanic-American poetry produced by authors born between 1965 and 1979. Taking into account the difficulty of achieving such an objective, *El decir y el vértigo*, beyond presenting a comprehensive Hispanic-American vision, manages to place within the reader's purview several young voices which, either by radical experimentation or by entries more closely tied to tradition, constitute the new poetic trailblazers of the region. In this sense, the selection is a useful tool in terms of familiarizing the reader with the works of the Argentine Fabián Casas, the Colombians Felipe García Quintero and Pascual Gaviria, the Chileans Germán Carrasco and Javier Bello, the Peruvian Paul Guillén, the Cuban Damaris Calderón and the Mexicans Luis Vicente de Aguinaga, Ernesto Lumbreras and Eduardo Padilla, among others. Likewise, the anthology represents a very important attempt to create links and establish a dialogue among the poets of the Hispanic-American world.

🔖 *Gaspar Orozco, Mexican Poet and Diplomat*

Diario de Argónida. *(Argolis Diary)*
Author: José Manuel Caballero Bonald
(Not Translated)

«The more I age the more life I have left», concludes one of the poems of *Argolis Diary (Diario de Argónida)*. Published when the Andalusian poet José Manuel Cabellero Bonald was over 70, this beautiful collection of crepuscular poems, full of experienced life, is a paean to fellow travelers «with little remorse and no abnegation,» to the geographic space the poet inhabits and where he declares himself. In short, this is a beautiful and happy elegy, the retelling and celebration of an existence —with errors no doubt— lived to the fullest.

🔖 *Lluís Agustí, Instituto Cervantes New York*

Filtraciones: poemas reunidos. *(Leaks: Collected Poems)*
Author: Hugo Gola
(Not Translated)

Filtraciones gathers almost 50 years of the literary oeuvre of the Argentine-Mexican poet Hugo Gola. Unconcerned by wavering literary trends, Gola has constructed, during the course of a half century, a solid poetic corpus whose distinctive traits are the concentration of sense, the intuition of detail and the essential gaze. Gola's poetry is a rigorous and profoundly human work which awaits discovery by the intelligent reader.
 Gaspar Orozco, Mexican Poet and Diplomat

Fuenteovejuna. *(Fuenteovejuna)*
Author: Lope de Vega
(Translated)

Spain's most prolific and greatest dramatist, Lope is said to have written more than 400 plays, many of which were comedies of the «capa y espada» (cloak and dagger) variety. *Fuenteovejuna* is a historical comedy, based on an actual happening, set against a background of historical fact, and peopled with peasants, royalty and a villanous nobleman. It is startling today for its use of a collective protagonist, the town of Fuenteovejuna, and its overt populism.
 Eduardo de Lamadrid, Trans-Lingual Communications Inc.

Las lenguas de diamante / Raíz salvaje. *(Diamond Tongues/Savage Root)*
Author: Juana de Ibarbourou
(Not Translated)

«I was hungry and thirsty for the most beautiful things in life. My hands were birds of the hunt.»
 Adan Griego, Stanford University Libraries

Libro de buen amor. *(The Book of Good Love)*
Author: Juan Ruiz, Arcipreste de Hita
(Translated)

The greatest of all Spanish «mester de clerecía» works and a comic masterpiece. The «buen amor» of the title refers to spiritual love as contrasted with «amor loco», carnal love. Although nominally favoring the former, the first-person narrator makes a concession to human frailty by dwelling at length on the latter. Juan Ruiz goes far beyond the theme of love, introducing a satire of medieval life and manners. Unforgettable characters are Trotaconventos, an old hag who is the hero's panderess and the prototype for all future go-betweens in Spanish literature, and Don Furón, the hero's rascally servant. Memorable also is the «parade of sausages» which anticipates Rabelais. This is a work by a good humored, jovial human being, yet who is also profoundly religious, charitable and tolerant. Quintessentially Spanish in his love of proverbs, little things and the anecdotal, he grounds his dreams and visions in real life.

🔊 *Eduardo de Lamadrid, Trans-Lingual Communications Inc.*

El libro del frío. *(The Book of Cold)*
Author: Antonio Gamoneda
(Not Translated)

Formed by «blocks of language» assembled with an exact balance of musicality and sense, the prose poems of this book enter unnamed territories where lightning illumines the earth for a second and eroticism reveals the body for a dark instant. At journey's end, since these poems are in many senses a voyage, we can say with the poet «now there is only light inside my eyes.» With *El libro del frío*, Antonio Gamoneda (Oviedo, 1931) has made a solid contribution to poetry in Spanish written on both sides of the Atlantic.

🔊 *Gaspar Orozco, Mexican Poet and Diplomat*

Luces de bohemia. *(Bohemian Lights)*
Author: Ramón María del Valle-Inclán
(Translated)

Valle-Inclán creates the theater of the grotesque, that is, the deformed and bizarre vision of reality, which according to the author himself was the best means of expressing the tragicomic Spanish reality of the early 20th century. The main character, a miserable poet called Max Estrella, lives out a bohemian night in Madrid and comes across a heterogeneous gallery of sad, tragic, and failed characters.

🔊 *Lluís Agustí, Instituto Cervantes New York*

No amanece el cantor. *(The Singer Does Not Awaken)*
Author: José Ángel Valente
(Not Translated)

A painful and ascetic work, yet full of beauty, from one of the most interesting poets of the end of 20th century, who always followed his own instincts. It disdain expressive excess; the poetic verb is handled with a religious, almost austere, reverence.

🔊 *Blanca Riestra, Instituto Cervantes Albuquerque*

Noticias del extranjero. *(News from Abroad)*
Author: Pedro Lastra
(Translated)

The first edition of *News from Abroad* was published a little over 25 years ago. During that period, this slim volume of poems has been reissued in numerous editions in various countries of the hemisphere. At the same time, slowly and patiently, new poems have been incorporated to its pages. The Chilean poet and academic Pedro Lastra (1932) locates the exact point between the immediate present and memory; from there, he names with absolute precision the beings and the absences which inhabit the days. For years a closely kept secret, *News from Abroad* is today, and justifiably so, a classic of Hispanic-American literature.
🔊 *Gaspar Orozco, Mexican Poet and Diplomat*

Nueve novísimos poetas españoles. *(Nine Innovative Spanish Poets)*
Author: J.M. Castellet, selec.
(Not Translated)

Critic and editor Josep Maria Castellet's selection in 1970 of the most innovative Spanish poets of the time has become a canonical work and created the idea of a group, if not united by generation or aesthetic, do share attitudes relative to language, poetic form and poetry itself. Included were poets Manuel Vázquez Montalbán, Antonio Martínez Sarrión, José María Álvarez, Félix de Azúa, Pere Gimferrer, Vicente Molina-Foix, Guillermo Carnero, Ana María Moix, and Leopoldo María Panero.
🔊 *Lluís Agustí, Instituto Cervantes New York*

Obra poética. *(Obra Poética, 1923-1969)*
Author: Jorge Luis Borges
(Translated)

Since the beginning, Jorge Luis Borges' poetical work seems to have been eclipsed by the fame garnered by his stories, yet the literary quality and worth of his poems is beyond dispute. As ingenious as his prose, and possessing the rhythms and melodies only known to a blind man, who instead of writing, recreates from memory, these poems have all the beauty and erudition of the stories, along with a musicality conducive to oral recitation.
🔊 *Lluís Agustí, Instituto Cervantes New York*

Obra poética. *(Poetic Works)*
Author: Íñigo López de Mendoza, Marqués de Santillana
(Translated)

This early Renaissance poet, critic, soldier and statesman introduced the sonnet form to Spanish literature. Yet his best lyrics are inspired by folk themes and forms derived from Galician poetry (*canciones, decires, serranillas* and *villancicos*). Santillana is distinguished for his delicate grace and sentiment expressed in simple form.
🔊 *Eduardo de Lamadrid, Trans-Lingual Communications Inc.*

Obra poética completa. *(Complete Poetry)*
Author: Jorge Carrera Andrade
(Not Translated)

This book gathers together the complete poetry of Jorge Carrera Andrade, considered—and rightly so—to be the best Ecuadorean poet of the 20th century. Carrera Andrade uses short forms that are largely free of Baroque mannerisms and close to the poetry of Asia, with a marvelous capacity for depicting landscape and impressions through visual metaphor. «Purify the world of shadowy thoughts—this is the essence. Let the eye ready its ship for a new discovery.»
🔊 *Lluís Agustí, Instituto Cervantes New York*

Obras completas: poesía completa y prosa selecta.
(Complete Works: Complete Poetry and Selected Prose)
Author: Alejandra Pizarnik
(Not Translated)

The brief life—cut short by her own hand—of this extraordinary Argentine poet has made her complete works, recommended here, fit into one volume. Despite their often tormented origin, her poems are clear, transparent, polished. «She who died because of her blue dress is singing. Imbued with death, she sings to the sun of her intoxication.»
🔊 *Lluís Agustí, Instituto Cervantes New York*

Obras escogidas. *(Selected Works)*
Author: San Juan de la Cruz
(Translated)

San Juan de la Cruz is the greatest of all the mystic poets and one of the greatest lyric poets the world has known. The humblest of men, he does not seek to describe the mystical experience itself. His rapturous spiritual joy overflows spontaneously in poetic lyricism, so that his verse does not directly state, but

rather, suggests and stimulates the imagination. The bucolic simplicity of his verses conceals untold depths of significance. Works such as *La subida del Monte Carmelo, Noche oscura del alma, Llama de amor viva,* and *Cántico espiritual* are masterpieces not only of Spanish, but also of world literature.
🔊 *Eduardo de Lamadrid, Trans-Lingual Communications Inc.*

Palabra sobre palabra: obra completa (1956-2001).
(Astonishing World: the Selected Poems of Ángel González, 1956-1986)
Author: Ángel González
(Translated)

Ángel González is a poet of profound social and human thinking and a skeptic from experience, but who, in spite of all, wants to keep writing. Perplexed and preoccupied by the world and the people who inhabit it in the absence of God, the poet has created beautiful texts which question reason and the relationship with the other, the «you», the self, time and death.
🔊 *Lluís Agustí, Instituto Cervantes New York*

Pic-Nic. El triciclo. El laberinto.
(Guernica, The Labyrinth, The Trycicle, Picnic on th Battlefield,
The Condemned Man's Bicycle)
Author: Fernando Arrabal
(Translated)

Cara Randall suggested this book saying Arrabal writes absurd drama (a bit like Ionesco). He's studied in literature classes. This book has 3 of his best in one volume.
🔊 *Millie Torrance, Sacramento Public Library*

La piel de toro. *(The Bull-hide = La Pell de Brau)*
Author: Salvador Espriu
(Translated)

Espriu's most important collection of poems and the one which establishes most clearly his voice of denunciation and admonition against Francoism.
🔊 *Jaume Martí Olivella, University of New Hampshire*

Poemas clandestinos. *(Clandestine Poems)*
Author: Roque Dalton
(Translated)

By one of the most recognized poets of El Salvador, in this collection of poems, the author in the voice of five imaginary poets conveys the political insight of his country.
🔊 *Alvaro Sanabria, San Francisco Public Library*

Poemas póstumos. *(Posthumous Poems)*
Author: Jaime Gil de Biedma
(Not Translated)

Jaime Gil de Biedma is one of the most influential poetic voices of the so-called Generation of 1950, also known as the Barcelona School. Gil de Biedma's poetry is autobiographical, notably realist in nature, and occasionally delves into social criticism. Posthumous collections, *Persons of the Verb* (*Las personas del verbo*) and *To Return* (*Volver*) are the beginning, and the best example, of the mode known as Poetry of Experience. Poetry of Experience and Poetry of Knowledge are the two fundamental currents of Spanish poetry at the end of the 20th century.
🔊 *Lluís Agustí, Instituto Cervantes New York*

Poesía. *(Coplas de Don Jorge Manrique)*
Author: Jorge Manrique
(Translated)

«Let from its dream the soul awaken, and reason mark with open eyes, the scene unfolding, How lightly life is taken, How cometh Death in stealthy guise, at last beholding; What swiftness hath the flight of pleasure that, once attained, seems nothing more than respite cold.» In 1476, upon his father's death, soldier and poet Jorge Manrique wrote the *Coplas*, some of the most beautiful verses ever written in Spanish, in which the idea and image of the passage of time, memory, the sadness which provokes happiness in remembrance will find a resolution difficult to surpass.
🔊 *Lluís Agustí, Instituto Cervantes New York*

Poesía. *(Ausiàs March: A Key Anthology)*
Author: Ausiàs March
(Translated)

The most important poet of medieval Catalan literature, he introduced Renaissance and Petrarchan forms and themes to the literatures of the Iberian peninsula.
🔊 *Jaume Martí Olivella, University of New Hampshire*

Poesía. *(Poetry)*
Author: Fray Luis de León
(Translated)

Like Garcilaso, Fray Luis de León's enduring fame rests on a handful of lyric poems, all of impeccable style and beauty. A master of the lira form, which he used in some of his best poems, «Vida retirada», «A Francisco Salinas», «Noche serena», etc., which are monuments to precision, technical perfection and depth of meaning. Idea and form, humanism and religion, appreciation of beauty and austerity of moral conception in him are completely blended. Hence the widely accepted view of Fray Luis as the incarnation of maximum harmony of the late Spanish Renaissance.

🔊 *Eduardo de Lamadrid, Trans-Lingual Communications Inc.*

Poesía selecta. *(Selected Poetry)*
Author: Ricardo Miró
(Not Translated)

Ricardo Miró is considered to be the best Panamanian poet of the 20th century. His perfectly rhymed verse is simply crafted, emotive and sincere.

🔊 *Lluís Agustí, Instituto Cervantes New York*

Poesía varia. *(Selected poetry)*
Author: Francisco de Quevedo
(Translated)

Although better known for his picaresque novels, Quevedo is nonetheless one of Spain's greatest poets. By temperament sarcastic, his pungent wit and mordant satire are evident in his verse, although he also wrote great metaphysical and love poems. His poems range from brief epigrams to long heroic poems, from the off-color to the deeply religious. He was an obdurate opponent of Culteranismo and Góngora, whom he satirized mercilessly. As an example of his power to ridicule, read the sonnet «A una nariz» (To a Nose) and as example of metaphysical love read the sonnet «Amor constante más alla de la muerte» (Constant Love Beyond Death), hailed by Dámaso Alonso as the greatest sonnet in Spanish literature.

🔊 *Eduardo de Lamadrid, Trans-Lingual Communications Inc.*

Poesías. *(Poems)*
Author: Luis de Góngora
(Translated)

The most important poetic texts of the Spanish Baroque period, of profound transcendence in the 17th century and renewed influence in the 20th century.

🔊 *Isaías Lerner, CUNY*

Poesías castellanas completas. *(Complete Castilian Poems)*
Author: Francisco de Aldana
(Not Translated)

The tragic figure of Captain Francisco de Aldana (1537-1578) exemplifies, as much as, or more than, Garcilaso de la Vega, the Renaissance ideal of the union of the sword and the pen. Deserving of much more attention than it currently

receives, the work of Francisco de Aldana astonishes the reader with the variety of its registers (which range from love to war, considering subtle spiritual questions along the way) and its clarity of tone. This edition, prepared by José Lara Garrido, allows us to appreciate Aldana as a master of the Castilian hendecasyllabic line, bringing into relief several of his sonnets and rima ottavas, as well as the tercets, both human and divine, of the «Epistle to Arias Montano».
 Gaspar Orozco, Mexican Poet and Diplomat

Poesías castellanas completas. *(Complete Castilian Poems)*
Author: Garcilaso de la Vega
(Translated)

«Corrientes aguas puras, cristalinas…» Thus flows Garcilaso's verse: pure, limpid, crystal clear. A consummate artist, his poems are models of form and beauty. This conscientious regard for perfection may account for his limited output: 38 sonnets, 5 songs, 3 eclogues, 2 elegies, one epistle and 8 coplas. He introduced Italian hendecasyllable verse and the metrical form known as the lira to Spanish verse. Yet this greatest of Spanish Renaissance poets is no mere formalist, and expresses the authentic, sincere sentiment of love with the melancholy and frustrated Platonism of the age.
 Eduardo de Lamadrid, Trans-Lingual Communications Inc.

Poesías liricas. *(Lyrical Poems)*
Author: Lope de Vega
(Translated)

Lope is also one of Spain's greatest lyrical poets, and wrote in all the forms of verse known in his day. With an extraordinary command of language and lyrical facility, he treated a universal array of themes, classical and contemporary, sacred and profane. Although at odds with Góngora, he did make some concessions to the prevaling vogue of Conceptismo.
 Eduardo de Lamadrid, Trans-Lingual Communications Inc.

Poeta en Nueva York. *(Poet in New York)*
Author: Federico García Lorca
(Translated)

This is probably one of the best book of poems written about New York City. Just read «Oda a Walt Whitman», and I think you'll agree.
 Ismael Alicea, The New York Public Library

Prosas profanas. *(Selected Writings)*
Author: Rubén Darío
(Translated)

Because it is, in the words of José Olivio Jiménez, «the insurmountable summit of all Modernist Aestheticism», and, as such, the signpost for all subsequent poetry in Spanish.
 Isaías Lerner, CUNY

Renaissance and Baroque Poetry of Spain.
Author: Elias L. Rivers
(Bilingual)

These are classical poems from the Renaissance and the Baroque. Used by FAU, this volume may be very helpful to American students since it is simultaneously translated into English.
 Guillermina Raffo Magnasco, St Thomas University

Residuos de los tiempos. *(Time's Residue)*
Author: Enrique Laguerre
(Not Translated)

On his first book of poems—published at the age of 94—Laguerre, one of the most renowned Puerto Rican authors of the 20th century, gives his readers his most intimate and lyric voice and opens them to his internal world of infancy, love, time, nation and nature.
 Nashieli Marcano, University of Akron

El retablo de las maravillas. *(The Magic Theatre)*
Author: Miguel de Cervantes
(Translated)

The theatrical genre known as the «interlude» is characterized by its brevity, contained in one act, and its comic or jocular nature. *The Magic Theatre (El retablo de las maravillas)* is one of the best known interludes by Miguel de Cervantes. It represents the history of some picaresque characters disguised as puppeteers who present to the audience a work plagued by wonders, yet wonders that can only be seen by old Christians (without Jewish blood) and children of legitimate marriage. Everything is a farce, there are no so called wonders and the spectators, as with the emperor's new clothes, will see what in reality does not exist for fear of public humiliation. A comedy of extraordinary contemporary relevance.
 Lluís Agustí, Instituto Cervantes New York

Rimas. *(Rhymes; and Legends)*
Author: Gustavo Adolfo Bécquer
(Translated)

We may see those poems as beautiful and simple but the poet knew that behind those «golondrinas», those same ones that will never come back, he could give us all deepness in simple thoughts. For the novide reader, the critical editions by Cátedra or Castalia can be very useful.

 Adan Griego, Stanford University Libraries

Romancero gitano. *(Gypsy Ballads)*
Author: Federico García Lorca
(Translated)

García Lorca's poetry is universal. These beautiful poems about life, death and gypsy superstitions are breathtaking.

Ismael Alicea, The New York Public Library

La rosa intemporal. *(The Timeless Rose)*
Author: Rafael Heliodoro Valle
(Not Translated)

This anthology brings together the best poetry by the Honduran writer, bibliographer and cultural ambassador Rafael Heliodoro Valle.

Lluís Agustí, Instituto Cervantes New York

El rumor del tiempo. *(The Murmur of Time)*
Author: César Antonio Molina
(Not Translated)

This book is a generous anthology of the poetry of César Antonio Molina, in which the reader encounters, in the words of Antonio Gamoneda, «outsized, muscular and revealing poetry», characterized by an unusual fusion of epic dimension and symbolic suggestion. For César Antonio Molina, writing is an archeological task in which remains are discovered and accumulated in order to decipher the enigma.

 Xosé Luis García Canido, Instituto Cervantes

Sonetos. *(Sonnets)*
Author: Luis de Góngora
(Translated)

The greatest and most complex poet of the late Golden Age, Góngora is synonomous with Culteranismo, a poetic school which relates mythological themes brimming with esoteric allusions and violent conceits (Conceptismo). Yet his sonnets, which are dense in imagery and metaphor, are distinguished by grace, charm, wit and vitality, and are much more accesible to modern readers than the lexically, syntactically and figuratively complex *Polifemo y Galatea* and the *Soledades*.
🔊 *Eduardo de Lamadrid, Trans-Lingual Communications Inc.*

Sóngoro cosongo. *(Sóngoro Cosongo)*
Author: Nicolás Guillén
(Not Translated)

The great Cuban poet Nicolás Guillén wrote that the following verses were born not composed: «In this land, mulata, of Africans and Spaniards, St. Barbara on one side and Changó on the other.» And it's true, Nicolás Guillén's poetry is a new poetry, a mestizo poetry, authentically musical, where the melody might be Spanish, but the rhythm is unmistakably African, a poetry which seems destined for song and for the dance, and which is based on the historical vindication of a color, the color black. *Sóngoro cosongo* is a book of poems which should be read aloud.
🔊 *Lluís Agustí, Instituto Cervantes New York*

Tala. *(Selected Poems)*
Author: Gabriela Mistral
(Translated)

Chilean poet Gabriela Mistral was the first Spanish American writer to win the Nobel Prize in Literature. But that is not the reason we are suggesting her work in this bibliography. Tala is an excellent book, genuine and passionate. Published in 1938, it was dedicated to the Basque children who suffered the hardships of the Spanish Civil War and of exile.
🔊 *Lluís Agustí, Instituto Cervantes New York*

Teatro español de vanguardia. *(Avant-Garde Spanish Theater)*
Author: Agustín Muñoz-Alonso López, ed.
(Not Translated)

The dramatic works of Federico García Lorca—some of them included in this selection—are undoubtedly the most widely known and popular of the Spanish experimental theater through the 1930's. Included along with them are works by other authors which remain unknown by the public-at-large, but which indisputably possess great literary and theatrical value: Corpus Barga, Antonio Espina, José Bergamín, Max Aub, José Bello and Luis Buñuel, Claudio de la Torre, Rafael Alberti, and Agustín Espinosa.

🔊 *Lluís Agustí, Instituto Cervantes New York*

Tesoros de la poesía en la lengua castellana.
(A Treasury of Castilian Poetry)
Author: Regino García-Badell
(Not Translated)

This book contains a splendid selection of Spanish and Latin American poetry. It provides a regular index, name index and first line verses index. It also includes a preface by the famous Spanish poet Rafael Alberti.

🔊 *Álvaro Sanabria, San Francisco Public Library*

Trilce. *(Trilce)*
Author: César Vallejo
(Translated)

This collection of poems both a bit sad and sweet is the companion piece to a previous volume and is marked by a boldness and profundity that will take away the reader's breath. Vallejo parts company with Surrealism to create his own expressive credo which only consists in surrendering to his own boundless and dark voice.

🔊 *Blanca Riestra, Instituto Cervantes Albuquerque*

Tuntún de pasa y grifería. *(Kinky-Haired and Frenzied Drumbeats)*
Author: Luis Palés Matos
(Not Translated)

This work represents classic Negro poetry at its best. Luis Palés Matos from Puerto Rico and Nicolás Guillén from Cuba are considered to be the best exponents of the Afro-Antillean genre. This work represents classic Afro-Antillean poetry at its best.

🔊 *Ismael Alicea, The New York Public Library*

Veinte poemas de amor y una canción desesperada.
(Twenty Love Poems and a Song of Despair)
Author: Pablo Neruda
(Translated)

This love poems written by the Nobel laureate in his early years are a must read.
🔊 *Ismael Alicea, The New York Public Library*

Versión celeste. *(Celestial Version)*
Author: Juan Larrea
(Not Translated)

A very beautiful yet anomalous book, which owes something to both Ultraism and Creationism, and more to Surrealism, written in almost all its entirety in French by a poet who sought the limits of language in his own reticence. It contains two of my favorite poems of all time, *Quarry (Flesh, my Dear Dynamite)* and *Reason (Succession of Sounds Moving to the Gleam)*, translated at one time by a very young Gerardo Diego.
🔊 *Blanca Riestra, Instituto Cervantes Albuquerque*

La vida es sueño. *(Life is a Dream)*
Author: Pedro Calderón de la Barca
(Translated)

Why a 17th century text? Because life is a dream and dreams are dreams as well. Calderón knew it then and it is still true today.
🔊 *Adan Griego, Stanford University Libraries*

NON FICTION

Los 1001 años de la lengua española. *(1001 Years of the Spanish Language)*
Author: Antonio Alatorre
(Not Translated)

How was our language born? How did it expand? How has it diversified? Alatorre answers these and other questions by narrating the history of Spanish language in an approachable style and using simple language. This book provides us with elements that allow us to understand the language's origins and to follow its development. And as the author says, to share in the magic of its history.
🔊 *Paloma Celis Carbajal, UW-Madison*

Artículos. *(Articles)*
Author: Mariano José de Larra
(Not Translated)

At the beginning of the convulsive and dramatic 19th century in Spain, a young writer laments the state of his sad, outmoded, uncultured country. The modern style and relevance of Mariano José de Larra's prose, in contrast to many of his contemporaries, is characterized by its precision, rhythm, humor and absence of pomposity. The marvelous journalistic chronicles of the young Larra, who died at the tender age of 27, allows us to approach the way of life and the problems of Spain in the 1830's, some of which are still with us to this day.
🔊 *Lluís Agustí, Instituto Cervantes New York*

Autobiografía de Federico Sánchez. *(The Autobiography of Federico Sánchez and the Communist Underground in Spain)*
Author: Jorge Semprún
(Translated)

Federico Sánchez was the alias by which Jorge Semprún was known within the Spanish Communist Party. Semprún was the grandson of Antonio Maura, the founder of the Spanish Right, and the son of an ambassador of the Second Spanish republic. At the end of the Civil War, the adolescent Semprún joins the French resistance and was detained by the Germans and sent to the Buchenwald camp. These memories are the way Semprún said goodbye to Federico Sánchez and accounted for his past in the Party.
🔊 *Lluís Agustí, Instituto Cervantes New York*

La bien plantada. *(A Comely Presence)*
Author: Eugeni d'Ors
(Not Translated)

Conceived as a philosophical novel, *La Bien Plantada*, published as a set of marginal notes in 1911, is the magnum opus of the most incisive and important Catalan intellectual of all time. In this work, *Xenius* (pseudonym of d'Ors), known to the Spanish reader for some of his famous marginal notes, describes the ideal of «Noucentisme» and his particular of vision of Catalonia personified in Teresa, a woman of semi-divine aspect and Greek-Mediterranean aesthetic, who incarnates the concepts of prudence, virtue and seductive and asexual discretion advocated by its author. A masterpiece which, unfortunately, has not been sufficiently appreciated, especially in Catalonia.
🔊 *Bernat Dedéu, Cadena Ser*

Biografía de un cimarrón. *(The Autobiography of a Runaway Slave)*
Author: Miguel Barnet
(Translated)

A disciple of Fernando Ortiz, Miguel Barnet makes an important contribution to the ethnographic literature of the Caribbean with this work, which has received international acclaim. In this biography, Esteban Montejo, a slave who managed to escape from the clutches of the odious «peculiar» institution, recounts his life and describes, perhaps without realizing it, Cuban society at the end of the 19th century and the beginning of the 20th century. A work of enormous importance to understand the cultural subtleties of the Hispanic Caribbean.
🔊 *Pedro Canó, Instituto Cervantes New York*

Borges profesor: curso de Literatura inglesa en la Universidad de Buenos Aires. *(Borges as Professor: Lectures in English Literature at the University of Buenos Aires)*
Author: Martín Arias, and Martín Hadis, eds.
(Not Translated)

A finely edited compilation of a course given by Borges on English literature, while not focusing on Spanish, does illustrate the way Borges approached the teaching of literature.
🔊 *Silvia Gil de Cwilich, Artist and Reader*

Breve historia de la literatura española.
(A Brief History of Spanish Literatura)
Author: Carlos Alvar, José-Carlos Mainer, and Rosa Navarro
(Not Translated)

Spanish university professors Carlos Alvar, José-Carlos Mainer, and Rosa Navarro are probably the greatest living authorities on Spanish literature, its history and criticism. An excellent and indispensable synthesis.
🔖 *Lluís Agustí, Instituto Cervantes New York*

Buscando un Inca: identidad y utopía en los Andes.
(In Search of an Inca: Identity and Utopia in the Andes)
Author: Alberto Flores Galindo
(Not Translated)

Eleven essays which relate various attempts to find utopias in Peru, from the search for an earthly paradise during the Conquest, through those in the colonial period culminating in Túpac Amaru's rebellion, and concluding in the 20th century with the millenarian guerrilla war carried by the Shining Path.
🔖 *Richard Heyer, Instituto Cervantes New York*

Campos de Níjar. *(The Countryside of Níjar)*
Author: Juan Goytisolo
(Translated)

New agricultural methods and tourism have greatly changed the people and the landscape of the province of Almería. Juan Goytisolo directed his socially acute eye and heart on a land whose people were prisoners of the scarcity of water and a lack of hope. It's incumbent on us to recall every so often that Spain only recently has ceased being a country characterized by poverty and emigration. Many changes for the good in a relatively short time have altered the essence and the image of a backward and unjust 19th century Spain which was perpetuated thanks to a long-lived dictatorship. A certain economic prosperity, a democracy not without difficulties and the opening of the country to the world are the keys to this radical change. These objectively positive changes in living standards and social freedoms, however, have produced the appearance of all manner of mountebank nouveau riches. When this happens it is good to recourse to recent social literature like *Campos de Níjar* in order to remember what we were until yesterday.
🔖 *Lluís Agustí, Instituto Cervantes New York*

Cancionero popular mexicano. *(Mexican Popular Songbook)*
Author: Mario Kuri-Aldana, and Vicente Mendoza Martínez
(Not Translated)

This two-volume edition published by Conaculta contains over one thousand song lyrics, many of them not only popular in Mexico but throughout Latin America and in other parts of the world. It includes biographical information and indexes by genre, authors and first line.
Alvaro Sanabria, San Francisco Public Library

Comentario de la Isagogé de Porfirio.
(Averroes Middle Commentary on Porphyry's Isagoge)
Author: Averroes
(Translated)

Born Abu-l-Walis Muhammad ibn Ahmad ibn Rusd in Cordoba in 1126, Averroes is the essential author of Hispano-Arabic philosophy and one of the most important commentators of Aristotle in the history of philosophy. Any of his commentaries is to be recommended, although the commentary on the *Book of the Compendium Exhibition of Isagogé of Porfirio* has received the most critical attention. In this work, Averroes traces the specific axes of his psychology, according to which the soul, as in Aristotle, is the primary faculty and entelechy of the human body. Elsewhere, the philosopher structures a passionate and complex schema of our cognitive activity in the cogitative, estimative, and judicative faculties. In parallel, Averroes committed himself, in what was a fiery polemic in his time, to affirming the existence of an agent of understanding, a capacity for reasoning common to all men and set apart from any reference to the divine, from which each human being develops his specific intelligence, called speculative understanding.
Bernat Dedéu, Cadena Ser

Comentarios Reales. *(The Royal Commentaries)*
Author: Inca Garcilaso de la Vega
(Translated)

Published in 1609, this remains the exemplary text of New World prose of the 16th and early 17th centuries. It introduced the South American world to Spanish readers and provided perspectives of both native inhabitants and privileged witnesses in Peru.
Isaías Lerner, CUNY

Cómo leer y escribir poesía. *(How to Read and Write Poetry)*
Author: Hugo Hiriart
(Not Translated)

With a confident and pleasant style, the celebrated Mexican novelist and playwright Hugo Hiriart offers a double introduction to poetry and to the Spanish language, addressed in principle to students of Spanish, but which may be enjoyed by all for its freshness, vigor and easily worn erudition. The guide uses key examples to examine poetic meter, rime, genres and themes, culminating with several chapters dedicated to awakening a taste for poetic writing in the reader. The book includes a bilingual dictionary interspersed within the text for English-speaking students With this volume, Hiriart has created an indispensable guide for North American libraries and bookstores.
Gaspar Orozco, Mexican Poet and Diplomat

Confieso que he vivido. *(Memoirs)*
Author: Pablo Neruda
(Not Translated)

This is a remarkable memoir in which Neruda writes about his journeys to exotic places, encounters with famous people and his love of poetry, life, art, nature and obviously his homeland.
Alvaro Sanabria, San Francisco Public Library

Contrapunto de género y raza en Puerto Rico.
(Puerto Rican Counterpoint: Gender and Race)
Author: Idsa E. Alegría Ortega, and Palmira N. Ríos, eds.
(Not Translated)

In light of the 2000 Census, where 85.5% of the population in Puerto Rico identified itself as white, this collection of essays contributes to the race debate by defining racism, its multiple ways of manifestation, its functionality and consequences.These articles pay special attention to the role of the Afro-Puerto Rican woman in the formation of national and international civil society, intersecting race and gender. Some of the topics covered include: history of black women in early 20th century education, racial ideology, Dominican migrant women, the racialization of women's work and national identity.
Nashieli Marcano, University of Akron

Conversación entre escritoras del Caribe Hispano: Tomo II.
(Conversation Between Women Writers of the Hispanic Caribbean: Volume II)
Author: Daisy Cocco De Filippis, and Sonia Rivera-Valdéz, eds.
(Not Translated)

The essays collected in this volume make an essential reference text for readers interested in the vision of contemporary Caribbean women writers. *Conversación* covers a wide range of literary genres, such as poetry, short story, novel and children literature, as well as dialogues that allow us to better understand their takes on the literary world.
🞕 *Nashieli Marcano, University of Akron*

Córdoba de los omeyas. *(The Cordoba of the Ummayids)*
Author: Antonio Muñoz Molina
(Not Translated)

An important history of Cordoba during the reign of the caliphates.
🞕 *Lynn Shirey, Harvard College Library*

El Criterio. *(The Criterion)*
Author: Jaume Balmes
(Translated)

El Criterio, 1843, remains the most important work of the philosopher Jaume Balmes. A thinker who has fallen in disgrace undoubtedly because of his profound religious convictions and his lifelong explicit defense of ecclesiastical authority, Balmes was nonetheless a very competent intellectual, an untiring follower of the Catalan empiricist tradition derived from Vives. In *The Criterion*, Balmes sets out the outlines of his epistemology (theory of knowledge), in which human knowledge emerges from the tripartite interaction between the conscience, «from which we apprehend real truths by means of reflection», the evidence, «which we find in ideal truths or propositions of an universal nature», and intellectual instinct, from which we may objectify our sensations and accept the real existence of exterior reality. With this theory, Balmes parted ways with the most naive realism and with post-Kantian rational idealism, opting clearly for an Aristotelian worldview. Also important and easier to read are some of his works addressing social problems, in which he defended the working class and distanced himself from political Machiavellianism.
🞕 *Bernat Dedéu, Cadena Ser*

Crítica y ficción. *(Criticism and Fiction)*
Author: Ricardo Piglia
(Not Translated)

Collection of essays covering mostly, but not exclusively Argentine writers. Truly a gem.
📖 *Silvia Gil de Cwilich, Artist and Reader*

Cruzando la frontera: la crónica implacable de una familia mexicana que emigra a Estados Unidos.
(Crossing Over: A Mexican Family on the Migrant Trail)
Author: Rubén Martínez
(Translated)

Award-winning journalist's poignant depiction of one Mexican family's courageous, multi-generational journey from Michoacán, Mexico to the U.S.
📖 *Patricia Cuesta, Los Angeles Public Library*

El cuaderno gris. *(The Gray Notebook)*
Author: Josep Pla
(Not Translated)

In this diary of youth, Catalan journalist Josep Pla (1897-1981) displays the pictorial prose which governed his subsequent prolific work, which extends to more than seventy volumes. Pla would write about the great events of the 20th century with the same aplomb and aversion to overstatement, whether from idealism or grandiloquence, which he evinces at 20 years of age in this work, considered to be his masterpiece.
📖 *Alfons Luna, AFP New York*

Cuadernos de Rusia. *(Russian Notebooks)*
Author: Dionisio Ridruejo
(Not Translated)

The politician, intellectual and poet Dionisio Ridruejo was one of the founders of the Spanish Falange, the extreme right revolutionary group which actively participated in the Francoist insurrection. In the recent aftermath of the Civil War, Ridruejo is one of the first voices to register disagreement with the new regime. Ridruejo resigns all his posts and departs for the Russian front with the Blue Division, the Spanish expeditionary force fighting alongside the Germans. In *Cuadernos de Rusia* he recounts his departure from Spain, his encounter with the Nazi reality and the discovery of Russia, while little by little his principles take other pathways.
📖 *Lluís Agustí, Instituto Cervantes New York*

Curso de redacción. Teoría y práctica de la composición y del estilo.
(Writing Course: Theory and Practice of Composition and Style)
Author: Gonzalo Martín Vivaldi
(Not Translated)

A great book which helps to resolve questions related to usage as well as to the composition of different types of texts.
◖ *Marko Miletich, Binghamton University (SUNY)*

El dardo en la palabra. *(The Dart in the Word)*
Author: Fernando Lázaro Carreter
(Not Translated)

Eminent Spanish language scholar and philologist Fernando Lázaro Carreter wrote a series of newspaper articles under the rubric *The Dart in the Word*. The objective of those articles was to correct usage and abusage of words in journalistic language, a task which at first glance might appear inquisitorial, but which was always effected with rigor, relevance, humor and irony, making those articles a perfect example of the joy of learning. The work recommended is a selection which has the same generic title as the newspaper articles. A second anthology was subsequently published as *The New Dart in the Word*. An enriching and enjoyable reading experience.
◖ *Lluís Agustí, Instituto Cervantes New York*

De Cristóbal Colón a Fidel Castro. El Caribe, frontera imperial.
(From Christopher Columbus to Fidel Castro: The Caribbean, Imperial Frontier)
Author: Juan Bosch
(Not Translated)

The historical magnum opus of this Dominican intellectual, once president of his country and a politician of great influence among Latin Americans who struggled against the military dictatorships of the 20th century. Juan Bosch sets out with dazzling clarity the history of exploitation suffered by the Caribbean since the arrival of the first Europeans until the triumph of the Fidel Castro's bearded guerillas in Cuba. This work is required reading for anyone wishing to learn the history and idiosyncrasy of the Caribbean as a region. The title echoes the work of another outstanding Caribbean figure, English in this case: Eric Williams, anti-colonial fighter and promoter of African independence movements.
◖ *Pedro Canó, Instituto Cervantes New York*

Del sentimiento trágico de la vida. *(The Tragic Sense of Life in Men and Nations)*
Author: Miguel de Unamuno
(Translated)

Essential writer of the Generation of 1898, Unamuno's philosophy is the product of the existential situation of Spain after the loss of its last colonies and describes the challenge of taking the country to an intellectual level comparable with the rest of Europe. The outlines of *Del sentimiento trágico de la vida* are sketched in insurmountable paradox which exists between the concepts of living and knowing. For Unamuno, human life is characterized by its complete irrationality, an irrationality which places it in irrepressible contradiction with the vital desires for knowledge innate in man. Elsewhere, Unamuno advocates for a complete differentiation between the spheres of reason and sentiment, two facets of the human being which are absolutely irreconcilable. According to Unamuno, life is synonymous with struggle, and more so, the life of an intellectual, a being who finds himself in the center of a struggle between reason and the needs of his appetite and will.
🔹 *Bernat Dedéu, Cadena Ser*

Diario del artista en 1956. *(Diary of an Artist in 1956)*
Author: Jaime Gil de Biedma
(Not Translated)

Jaime Gil de Biedma had left instructions for the publication after his death of his *Diario del artista en 1956*. It was the same work which had appeared in 1974 as *Diary of a Gravely Ill Artist*, but this last version was complete and uncensored. Terminally ill with AIDS, Gil de Biedma wanted to leave a record and chronicle of his personal and literary experiences, of friendships and sexual adventures in Spain and the Philippines throughout those months. An excellent personal chronicle by one of the best Spanish poets of the 20th century.
🔹 *Lluís Agustí, Instituto Cervantes New York*

El ensayo hispanoamericano del siglo XX.
(The Hispanic-American Essay in the 20th Century)
Author: John Skirius, ed.
(Not Translated)

Undergoing consecutive and necessary editions, this anthology has become indispensable and a required recommendation. Among the authors included in this excellent selection of the best 20th century Hispanic-American essays are Alfonso Reyes, Fernando Ortiz, José Carlos Mariategui, Enrique Anderson Imbert,

Alejo Carpentier, Octavio Paz and Carlos Monsiváis. A sometimes forgotten genre in Hispanic-American literary histories, but certainly not due to a lack of superior writers and profound works, comparable to the highest essayistic achievements at the international level.
❧ *Lluís Agustí, Instituto Cervantes New York*

Enseñar a traducir: metodología en la formación de traductores e intérpretes. *(Learning to Translate. Methodology for Training Translators and Interpreters)* Author: Amparo Hurtado Albir *(Not Translated)*

A very practical book which presents a course of study for the teaching of translation.
❧ *Marko Miletich, Binghamton University (SUNY)*

La esclavitud del negro en Santo Domingo. *(Negro Slavery in Santo Domingo)* Author: Carlos Esteban Deive *(Not Translated)*

Slave relations in the Spanish colony of Santo Domingo were very different from those which prevailed in great part of the French Caribbean, in the English-speaking Caribbean and in Cuba, until the late abolition of slavery in the largest of the Antilles. The author analyzes those relations with an economic perspective, and as a serious researcher, committed to the exposition of historical truth.
❧ *Pedro Canó, Instituto Cervantes New York*

Escrituras de Frida Kahlo. *(Frida by Frida)* Author: Frida Kahlo *(Translated)*

Diego Rivera's personal secretary compiled these very personal and insightful writings by Kahlo on the topic of her private life, her painting, her husband, family and friends.
❧ *Patricia Cuesta, Los Angeles Public Library*

España en su historia. *(The Spaniards: An Introduction to Their History)* Author: Américo Castro *(Translated)*

A controversial look at Spanish history.
❧ *Patricia Figueroa, Brown University Library*

Federico García Lorca. *(Federico García Lorca)*
Author: Ian Gibson
(Translated)

Certainly the most complete biography of the great Lorca. It is also a biography of Spain at a great time of crisis. Gibson himself revised and translated the English edition published in 1989.
🔖 *Adan Griego, Stanford University Libraries*

Franco, Caudillo de España. *(Franco, a Biography)*
Author: Paul Preston
(Translated)

An extensive and well-documented biography of General Francisco Franco, the dictator who governed Spain between 1939 and 1975. An excellent work of historical and political research, as well as a sociological and psychological study of the public and private lives of the Caudillo.
🔖 *Lluís Agustí, Instituto Cervantes New York*

Hablando seriamente: textos y pretextos para conversar y discutir.
(Talking Seriously: Texts and Pretexts for Conversation and Discussion)
Author: Rubén Benítez, and Paul C. Smith
(Not Translated)

This book contains short essays. For example, some of the topics here included are: The Influence of Television on Students, Drugs, Alcohol, Sex Inequality, Animal Extinction, etc. All of these topics include vocabulary and comprehension practice.
🔖 *Guillermina Raffo Magnasco, St Thomas University*

Las historias prohibidas del Pulgarcito.
(Prohibited Stories of El Salvador: America's Little Thumb)
Author: Roque Dalton
(Not Translated)

Using Gabriela Mistral's phrase, «El Salvador, America's little thumb.» as a point of departure, poet and journalist Roque Dalton creates an absorbing essay about the history and reality of America's little thumb.
🔖 *Lluís Agustí, Instituto Cervantes New York*

Huesos en el desierto. *(Bones in the Desert)*
Author: Sergio González Rodríguez
(Not Translated)

Product of intensive research and study, *Bones in the Desert* is probably the best investigative book written about the disappearance of some 300 young women from the vicinity of Ciudad Juarez, Mexico. With documentary and critical precision, González Rodríguez analyzes in detail the process of social and political disintegration which this border city has undergone, and which permitted that said crimes be committed in an alarming environment of impunity. A lucid chronicle, written with determination, courage and intelligence, *Bones in the Desert* offers readers horrifying testimony about a horrifying event, a critical limit for Mexican society. González Rodríguez has written a hard but necessary book, and as such it should not go unnoticed. No wonder Roberto Bolaño used it as inspiration and documentary source in the creation of his latest novel, *2666*.
🔌 *Gaspar Orozco, Mexican Poet and Diplomat*

Introducción a la traductología. *(Introduction to Translation Theory)*
Author: Gerardo Vázquez-Ayora
(Not Translated)

A fundamental book for beginners in the field of translation theory with a linguistic vision based on the ideas of generative transformational grammar.
🔌 *Marko Miletich, Binghamton University (SUNY)*

La isla que se repite.
(The Repeating Island: The Caribbean and the Postmodern Perspective)
Author: Antonio Benítez Rojo
(Translated)

The author's most outstanding work, it uses essays, narrative, chaos theory and postmodern theory in an attempt to comprehend the Caribbean soul. This unique book dazzled American academics, was praised by John Updike and received the Pushcart Prize.
🔌 *Fernando Velázquez Medina, Writer and Journalist*

Juan Pérez Jolote: biografía de un tzotzil.
(Juan the Chamula: An Ethnological Re-Creation of the Life of a Mexican Indian)
Author: Ricardo Pozas
(Translated)

This is an ethnological re-creation of the life of a Mexican Tzotzil Indian. A daily account of the life, times and changes of the indigenous.
🔌 *Angélica Hurtado-Gracia, LAPL*

El laberinto de la soledad.
(The Labyrinth of Solitude, the Other Mexico, and other Essays)
Author: Octavio Paz.
(Translated)

A work that explores the psyche of the Mexican people in relation to the United States.
🔍 *Angela Encinas, San Bernardino Public Library*

El largo viaje. *(The Long Voyage)*
Author: Jorge Semprún
(Translated)

Jorge Semprún (1923) lived out his adolescence between two wars, the Spanish Civil War and World War II. Convinced that Hitler's defeat would lead to Franco's fall, this grandson of Prime Minister Antonio Maura, and Minister of Culture between 1988 and 1991, joined the French Resistance, and at 19 years of age was imprisoned in the Buchenwald death camp. His experience there was recounted in *The Long Journey* (*El largo viaje*), the best testimony by a Spaniard of the Nazi extermination program.
🔍 *Alfons Luna, AFP New York*

Larra, anatomía de un dandy. *(Larra: Anatomy of a Dandy)*
Author: Francisco Umbral
(Not Translated)

Very often the opinions, attitudes and manner of the Spanish writer and journalist Francisco Umbral have concealed from authors and readers an astounding reality, which is that here is one of the greatest contemporary Spanish writers of prose, gifted with an excellent and original literary register, and with a prodigious capacity for observing the cultural and academic worlds. This superb essay about a fellow writer and journalist from the 19th century, Mariano José de Larra, another literary phenomenon, provides the necessary proof.
🔍 *Lluís Agustí, Instituto Cervantes New York*

Latinoamérica: su civilización y su cultura.
(Latin America: Culture and Civilization)
Author: Eugenio Chang-Rodríguez
(Not Translated)

This book deals with key historical and cultural events that occurred in Latin America. Each chapter includes comprehension exercises and a bilingual vocabulary.
🔍 *Guillermina Raffo Magnasco, St Thomas University*

Lo esencial en la ortografía. *(Essential Orthography)*
Author: Francisco Alvero Francés
(Non Translated)

Contains a long list of homophones and a presentation of the principal orthographic rules which govern the use of our consonants.
🦞 *Marlenys Villamar, Professor*

Manual de traducción inglés/castellano. *(The English/Spanish Translation Manual)*
Author: Gabriel López Guix, and J. Minnet Wilkinson
(Not Translated)

A very skillful comparative analysis of the English and Spanish languages which stresses the syntactical, morphological and punctuation aspects of each language.
🦞 *Marko Miletich, Binghamton University (SUNY)*

Manuel Azaña: entre el mito y la leyenda.
(Manuel Azaña: Between Myth and Legend)
Author: Ángeles Egido León
(Not Translated)

A serene and rigorous study about one of the most important figures of the Second Spanish Republic, Manuel Azaña. President of the Government and until the last days of the Civil War, President of the Republic, Azaña died in exile in Montauban, France in 1940. His political and moral figure undoubtedly transcended his death and informed the intellectual and political climate during the years of Francoism and during the Transitional Period.
🦞 *Lluís Agustí, Instituto Cervantes New York*

Memoria de la melancolía. *(Melancholy Memories)*
Author: María Teresa León
(Not Translated)

María Teresa León recounts her personal, political, cultural and literary experiences. An exquisite novelist of the poetic Generation of 1927, she shared her life with the poet Rafael Alberti, to whom she was also united by literature and political struggle. *Memoria de la melancolía* is one of the most beautiful prose works ever written about the era of the Republic, the Civil War and exile.
🦞 *Lluís Agustí, Instituto Cervantes New York*

Memorias. *(Memoirs)*
Author: Carlos Barral
(Not Translated)

Carlos Barral was undoubtedly one of the most important Spanish editors of the 20th century, besides being a first-rate reader and critic. A complex and difficult poet, he is however an excellent prose stylist. His memoirs are divided into three volumes: *Years of Punishment,* which relates his childhood, adolescence and young adulthood in the years following the Civil War; *The Inexcusable Years,* which relates his experiences during the 1950's; and *The Fleeting Hours,* which closes the cycle with his mature adult life, with special reference to his cultural and literary life.
Lluís Agustí, Instituto Cervantes New York

Memorias. *(Memoirs)*
Author: Josep Maria de Sagarra
(Not Translated)

One of the greatest literary memoirs of the Catalan and Spanish 20th century. First published in 1957, this delectable, rich and entertaining work provides insights into Catalan society and literature at the end of the 19th century and during the first half of the 20th.
Lluís Agustí, Instituto Cervantes New York

Misión del bibliotecario y otros ensayos afines. *(The Mission of the Librarian)*
Author: José Ortega y Gasset
(Translated)

In the inaugural conference of proceedings of the 11th International Congress of Libraries and Bibliography, celebrated jointly in Madrid and Barcelona in May 1935, Spanish philosopher José Ortega y Gasset gave a lecture, or to be more exact, read his essay *The Mission of the Librarian,* a text which in spite of the passage of 70 years continues to be of enormous interest and relevance. Required reading for librarians and recommended for all library users.
Lluís Agustí, Instituto Cervantes New York

Mitología y artes prehispánicas de las Antillas.
(Pre-Hispanic Mythology and Arts of the Antilles)
Author: José Juan Arrom
(Not Translated)

José Juan Arrom is one of the most important figures in pre-Hispanic studies in the Caribbean. In this work, his expert eye falls on the relationships between mythology and the arts of the indigenous peoples of the archipelago and explains some of those links.
Pedro Canó, Instituto Cervantes New York

Morir en el intento. *(Dying to Cross)*
Author: Jorge Ramos
(Translated)

This is an important work which addresses the problem of human smuggling across the Mexican border.
🔊 *Millie Torrance, Sacramento Public Library*

La mujer negra en la literatura puertorriqueña: cuentística de los setenta.
(Black Women in Puerto Rican Literature: Short Stories of the 1970s)
Author: Marie Ramos Rosado
(Not Translated)

In addition to being a rigorous investigative project, the text is a personal testimonial on literature, describing it as a fertile space of social struggles and as intellectual and human catharsis. In her effort to understand aesthetic and literary processes, Ramos Rosado establishes relationships between «negritude» and feminism.
🔊 *Nashieli Marcano, University of Akron*

Naufragios y Comentarios. *(Chronicle of the Narváez Expedition)*
Author: Alvar Núñez Cabeza de Vaca
(Translated)

This account of the journeys of Spanish explorer Alvar Núñez Cabeza de Vaca throughout northern North America, and later throughout the southernmost regions of the continent, evinces, beyond its immense historical importance, literary and human merit of the first order. In clear and precise prose, Alvar Núñez details the fortunes (less of these) and misfortunes (more of these) of his wanderings in the almost unfathomable distances of the southern United States and northern Mexico, collecting his incisive observations about the regions and the inhabitants encountered along the way. *Naufragios y Comentarios* is an eyewitness testimony to one of the great enterprises of the human spirit.
🔊 *Gaspar Orozco, Mexican Poet and Diplomat*

La noche de Tlatelolco. *(Massacre in Mexico)*
Author: Elena Poniatowska
(Translated)

This book chronicles the events of the student protests in October of 1968 in Mexico City that resulted in the massacre of more than 300 persons.
🔊 *Teresa Chapa, University of North Carolina at Chapel Hill*

La ola latina: cómo los hispanos están transformando la política en los Estados Unidos. *(The Latin Wave: How Hispanics are Transforming Politics in the United States)*
Author: Jorge Ramos
(Translated)

A powerful, well-documented analysis of why the growing numbers of Latinos in the United States can no longer be ignored and how they are changing the face of the country.
 Patricia Cuesta, Los Angeles Public Library

Oráculo manual y arte de prudencia.
(The Art of Worldly Wisdom: A Pocket Oracle)
Author: Baltasar Gracián
(Translated)

A collection of 300 aphorisms or maxims about wisdom, by one of the greatest prose stylists in the Spanish language. In them can be discerned a whole plan of conduct for life which, four hundred years later, seems surprisingly modern.
 Eduardo Lago, Instituto Cervantes New York

La orgía perpetua. *(The Perpetual Orgy: Flaubert and Madame Bovary)*
Author: Mario Vargas Llosa
(Translated)

Vargas Llosa is my favorite writer of the so called Latin American Boom (a «discovery» of Latin American literature as paradoxical as the «discovery» of America). *The Perpetual Orgy (La orgía perpetua)* is a critical essay on Madame Bovary of exceptional brilliance. Vargas Llosa elucidates the novel's framework by means of a close and passionate reading. The critic's passion for the work does not cloud his judgment, on the contrary, passion leads to illumination. His reading provides an example of how to read and evaluate a literary work: without meanness and with the same generosity of spirit and passion that informs the source text.
Silvia Gil de Cwilich, Artist and Reader

Los orishas en Cuba. *(The Orishas in Cuba)*
Author: Natalia Bolívar Aróstegui
(Not Translated)

For those interested in Afro-Caribbean religions, this book is a must read. The author touches on the entire pantheon of the Cuban divinities-orishas and on her journey leaves us with a fascinating description of the beliefs and aspirations of the faithful. An important work in the field of comparative religion studies.
Pedro Canó, Instituto Cervantes New York

El país bajo mi piel. *(The Country Under my Skin)*
Author: Gioconda Belli
(Translated)

A fascinating autobiography by Nicaragua's most important contemporary writer. Belli chronicles very personal accounts of her life as well as her active participation in the Sandinista revolution.
🔹 *Teresa Chapa, University of North Carolina at Chapel Hill*

El país de cuatro pisos y otros ensayos.
(The Four Story Country and Other Essays)
Author: José Luís González
(Not Translated)

González delineates the stages of Puerto Rican culture and nation as a reflex of ongoing power relations within the colonial society and under the impact of foreign domination. *El país de cuatro pisos* is to the 1980's what «Insularismo», the classic essay by Antonio Pedreira, was in the 1930's.
🔹 *Nashieli Marcano, University of Akron*

Panorama de la prensa: temas contemporáneos del mundo hispano.
(Press Overview: Contemporary Themes of the Hispanic World)
Author: Juan Kattan Ibarra
(Not Translated)

These are articles from newspapers in the Hispanic World. These articles encourage students' interaction in class in the form of debates. The articles also contain vocabulary explanation as well as comprehension practice.
🔹 *Guillermina Raffo Magnasco, St Thomas Universuty*

Pasando página: autores y editores en la España democrática.
(Turning the Page: Authors and Editors in Democratic Spain)
Author: Sergio Vila-Sanjuán
(Not Translated)

The Spanish cultural journalist Sergio Vila-Sanjuán offers an interesting tour of the editorial and literary world in Spain from the Transitional Period to the present. A welcoming yet well-researched work, it contains valuable information necessary to understand the ins and outs of the industry: names, firms, the much discussed world of literary prizes. It also includes some interesting informational charts about Spanish publishing houses.
🔹 *Lluís Agustí, Instituto Cervantes New York*

La pasión por los libros: un acercamiento a la bibliofilia.
(A Passion for Books: An Approach to Bibliophilia)
Author: Francisco Mendoza Díaz-Maroto
(Not Translated)

Spanish bibliophile Francisco Mendoza Díaz-Maroto intends to transmit his passion for the printed books in this friendly, and occasionally diverting, work. Even though the reader might not share that passion, in the end he or she will understand the fever which consumes book collectors. An erudite and entertaining work.
● *Lluís Agustí, Instituto Cervantes New York*

Persona non grata.
(Persona Non Grata: A Memoir of Disenchantment with the Cuban Revolution)
Author: Jorge Edwards
(Translated)

Writer Jorge Edwards (1931) was the first diplomatic envoy from Salvador Allende's Chile to Fidel Castro's Cuba. Persona non grata is the memoir of the difficult coexistence between Edwards and the Cuban Revolution which would end with his expulsion from the island. This is the first great critique by a Latin American intellectual of the authoritarianism of a regime which was the time the object of widespread idealization.
● *Alfons Luna, AFP New York*

Perspectivas culturales de Hispanoamérica.
(Hispanic American Cultural Perspectives)
Author: Juan Kattan Ibarra
(Not Translated)

The focus of this book is on crucial Latin American historical events. This book will provide the student with an overall picture of the most important historical events.
● *Guillermina Raffo Magnasco, St Thomas University*

El pez en en el agua: memorias. *(A Fish in the Water: A Memoir)*
Author: Mario Vargas Llosa
(Translated)

Mario Vargas Llosa relates his childhood, adolescent and young adulthood memories, alternating chapter by chapter, with his experiences as a candidate for the presidency of Peru, as wells as his justifications for said candidacy. Apart from the brilliant and precise style for which he is known, the work offers the added incentive of discovering those personal experiences which informed novels such as *La ciudad y los perros (The City and the Dogs)*, *La casa verde (The Green House)*, and *La tía Julia y el escribidor (Aunt Julia and the Scriptwriter)*.
● *Lluís Agustí, Instituto Cervantes New York*

Las primeras representaciones gráficas del indio americano, 1493-1523.
(The First Graphic Representations of American Natives, 1493-1523)
Author: Ricardo E. Alegría
(Not Translated)

What place did America occupy in the European imagination of the late 15th century and early 16th century? Professor Ricardo E. Alegría, one of the most prominent figures in Caribbean ethnological studies, follows the clues left to us by witnesses of the first contacts between Europeans and Americans in the Antillean islands. A great bibliographical contribution and an opportunity to take the measure of this beloved Puerto Rican intellectual.
🔍 *Pedro Canó, Instituto Cervantes New York*

La Raza Cómica: del sujeto en Puerto Rico.
(The Comic Race: About the Subject in Puerto Rico)
Author: Rubén Ríos Ávila
(Not Translated)

A collected literary and cultural criticism by a prize-winning acclaimed writer, *La raza cómica* is an intelligent and intense model for rethinking culture. Informed by an openly gay sensibility, Ríos Ávila's studies offer a reflection of how the phantasmagoric presence defines the subject. Themes include Palés, the Caribbean as cabaret, and Ramos Otero.
🔍 *Nashieli Marcano, University of Akron*

La rebelión de las masas. *(The Revolt of the Masses)*
Author: José Ortega y Gasset
(Translated)

Of all the philosophical works written in Spanish, *The Revolt of the Masses* (*La rebelión de las masas*) is perhaps the one which has been translated more often and has had more intellectual influence on a worldwide scale. This is not mere chance; the book, written in 1926 and published four years later, projects onto a more ambitious global setting the intuitions which its author had sketched in *Invertebrate Spain* (*La España invertebrada*), from which society is structured in reciprocal action between the masses and a select minority of citizens. This interaction allows society to evolve, if the minorities are virtuous classes who should guide the general will of the masses toward good actions. In *The Revolt of the Masses*, Ortega y Gasset anticipated something that at the time few had recognized, namely, the characterization of a new paradigm of the mass-man, a depersonalized being who only thinks of the free expansion and fulfillment of his primary needs and desires and who does not express any gratitude for the historic and social conditions which have made possible his well-being as well as the political normalcy of his existence. A man, who failing to appeal to a higher and virtuous exemplar which he can imitate, becomes easy prey for totalitarian regimes and dictatorships. A paradigm, which, as World War II demonstrated, has survived in our time and perhaps is even more dangerous.

🔊 *Bernat Dedéu, Cadena Ser*

Relación acerca de las antigüedades de los indios.
(An Account of the Antiquites of the Indians: Chronicles of the New World Encounter)
Author: Ramón Pané, Fray, and José Juan Arrom, ed.
(Translated)

This *Account...* was the first document written in the Americas by a European. Ramón Pané, a Catalan friar of the order of St. Jerome, was asked by Columbus to describe the Taino culture he had found in the island of Hispaniola. This is a document of inestimable value for the study of the Caribbean during the time of the encounter between cultures. Lost for centuries until discovered and made public by the researcher José Juan Arrom, in a scholarly edition under his supervision.

🔊 *Pedro Canó, Instituto Cervantes New York*

Respuesta a Sor Filotea. *(The Answer: Including a Selection of Poems)*
Author: Sor Juana Inés de la Cruz
(Translated)

In a tone of utter humility, Sister Juana's letter provides one of the best defenses of the right of women to use their intellect. The autobiographical passages that Sister Juana includes make this an enjoyable reading experience, and also contain much information about life in Mexico during the colonial period.

🔊 *Paloma Celis Carbajal, UW-Madison*

El río: novelas de caballería. *(The River: Novels of Chivalry)*
Author: Luis Cardoza y Aragón
(Not Translated)

El río is not only a memoir, but also a hodgepodge of erudition, a crossroads. In this book, the restless Guatemalan traveler, writer and intellectual compiles a variety of materials which in the end form a complete and fascinating portrait.

🔊 *Lluís Agustí, Instituto Cervantes New York*

Teoría y práctica de la traducción. *(Translation Theory and Practice)*
Author: Valentín García Yebra
(Not Translated)

A basic text for all students of translation, expounding a linguistic and comparative approach to translation.
🦅 *Marko Miletich, Binghamton University (SUNY)*

Traducción y traductología. Introducción a la traductología.
(Translation and Translation Studies. An Introduction to the Study of Translation)
Author: Amparo Hurtado Albir
(Not Translated)

An excellent and all-encompassing compilation of translation theories with special emphasis placed on modern theories.
🦅 *Marko Miletich, Binghamton University (SUNY)*

Traducción: literatura y literalidad.
(Translation: Literature and Literalness)
Author: Octavio Paz
(Not Translated)

A lucid exposition of the philosopher's theories which highlights his vision of literary translation as adaptation.
🦅 *Marko Miletich, Binghamton University (SUNY)*

Tragicomedia mexicana: la vida en México de 1940 a 1970.
(Mexican Tragicomedy: Life in Mexico between 1940 and 1970)
Author: José Agustín
(Not Translated)

A very well-documented story that relates, with irony and humor, the great political and economic events of recent years, and also comments on social life, film, the mambo, the 1985 earthquake, the first feminists and Mexican rock.
🦅 *Richard Heyer, Instituto Cervantes New York*

La travesía de Enrique. *(Enrique's Journey)*
Author: Sonia Nazario
(Translated)

The compelling, illuminating account of a young Honduran boy who faces insurmountable odds to reunite with his immigrant mother in the U.S. is told in vivid detail by an award-winning *Los Angeles Time* journalist.
🦅 *Patricia Cuesta, Los Angeles Public Library*

Travesías. *(Crossings)*
Author: Jaime Salinas
(Not Translated)

Editor Jaime Salinas tells the story of a different exile, of those who left Spain as children because of the Civil War. Son of the poet Pedro Salinas, Jaime Salinas covers thirty years of his life, and especially the formative years: from childhood in Madrid and the Valencian coast, the departure toward France and Algeria when war breaks out, his adaptation to life in North America, his intervention in the World War. The cycle closes when he returns to a Spain which feels strange to him and which he does not know. An interesting portrait of another exile.

🔍 *Lluís Agustí, Instituto Cervantes New York*

Las venas abiertas de América Latina.
(Open Veins of Latin America: Five Centuries of the Pillage of a Continent)
Author: Eduardo Galeano
(Translated)

This is a prominent book indispensable for any Spanish book collection. It presents a historical, political, social and economic survey written in an outstanding narrative.

🔍 *Alvaro Sanabria, San Francisco Public Library*

Vida moderna hispana. *(Modern Hispanic Life)*
Author: James W. Brown
(Not Translated)

This book contains a series of interviews to people from different cultures. It is an important learning source to enhance multicultural awareness in our students.

🔍 *Guillermina Raffo Magnasco, St Thomas University*

Visión de Anáhuac y otros ensayos. *(Vision of Anáhuac and Other Essays)*
Author: Alfonso Reyes
(Not Translated)

The essays of this collection —with *Vision of Anáhuac* as a guidepost— offer an example of Alfonso Reyes' extraordinary and superb prose, his rich effects, his colorful palette, his musicality. Reyes is to prose in Spanish what Darío was to poetry: the renovation of the language, the cheerful confirmation of the capacity of the words themselves to go far beyond. The river of images shine with a hypnotic force, with the shine of a real jewel, a pleasure for the senses and intellect of the reader.

🔍 *Lluís Agustí, Instituto Cervantes New York*

Vituperio (y algún elogio) de la errata.
(Censure (and Some Acclaim) of Errata)
Author: José Esteban
(Not Translated)

Errata are those writing errors which appear in the least expected places of a printed work. While sometimes they may make the work hilarious, they rarely improve on it. Editors, proofreaders and typographers are always on the lookout for this nightmare in books, magazines and newspapers. In this work, more than just a mere listing of errors, José Esteban takes us on a delightful, friendly and frequently jocular tour of errata appearing in Spanish publications.
🔍 *Lluís Agustí, Instituto Cervantes New York*

Vivir para contarla. *(Living to Tell the Tale)*
Author: Gabriel García Márquez
(Translated)

The complete works of Gacía Márquez are a must but the first volume of his memoirs is another masterpiece. Donna Seaman of the *Booklist* wrote in her review: «Invaluable in its personal and cultural history, and triumphant in its compassion and artistry, García Márquez's portrait of himself as a young writer is as revelatory and powerful as his fiction.»
🔍 *Alvaro Sanabria, San Francisco Public Library*

Vudú y magia en Santo Domingo.
(Voodoo and Magic in the Dominican Republic)
Author: Carlos Esteban Deive
(Not Translated)

A classic work about the controversial subject of Dominican popular religion and its relationship to Haitian voodoo. Deive describes the rituals, identifies the similarities and differences between both complex ritual traditions, and explains the impressive cosmology which informs Dominican religious practice.
🔍 *Pedro Canó, Instituto Cervantes New York*

REFERENCE

50.000 nombres para su bebé. *(50,000 Names for Your Baby)*
Author: Equipo Editorial
(Not Translated)

This book contains an extensive list of baby names including information on etymology, personality, historical background, and versions in other languages.
🔍 *Alvaro Sanabria, San Francisco Public Library*

Antología crítica del cine español: 1906-1995.
(Critical Anthology of Spanish Film: 1906-1995)
Author: Julio Pérez Perucha, ed.
(Not Translated)

From close to 6,000 titles which comprise the history of Spanish film to date, a group of academic and film researchers selected 305 films considered key to the history of our cinematographic tradition and provided an interesting critical study of each selection. This work was sponsored by the Spanish Association of Film Historians. Indispensable for both libraries and film buffs.
🔍 *Lluís Agustí, Instituto Cervantes New York*

Cine argentino. *(Argentine Film)*
Author: Claudio España, ed.
(Not Translated)

This work can be currently divided into three others: *Argentine Film under Democracy: 1983-1993*; *Argentine Film: Industry and Classicism, 1933-1956*; and *Argentine Film: Modernity and the Avant-Garde, 1957-1983*. Sponsored by the National Fund for the Arts and written by the most prominent historians of Argentine film, the work is organized by themes and plots, and the films are considered in the context of Argentine history. An excellent analytical work, indispensable for both libraries and film buffs.
🔍 *Lluís Agustí, Instituto Cervantes New York*

Cine documental en América Latina. *(Documentary Film in Latin America)*
Author: Paulo Antonio Paranaguá
(Not Translated)

This resource contains extensive (6-20 page) biographies of fifteen Latin American documentary film makers, as well as a chronological list of major films in this genre from 1921 to 2002. Also included is a selection of essays on the subject and a thirty-page bibliography of related sources.
🔍 *Teresa Chapa, University of North Carolina at Chapel Hill*

Diccionario crítico etimológico castellano e hispánico.
(Critical and Etymological Castilian and Hispanic Dictionary)
Author: Joan Corominas
(Not Translated)

This is the etymological dictionary par excellence of the Spanish language. In its six volumes, the reader will be able to find not only the origin of a given word, but also documented examples of how the word was originally used and its subsequent evolution.

🔊 *Paloma Celis Carbajal, UW-Madison*

Diccionario de autores latinoamericanos.
(Dictionary of Latin American Authors)
Author: César Aira
(Not Translated)

César Aira is a well-known Argentine novelist, translator, dramatist and essayist. Two facts about this work are worth reporting: Aira specifically dedicates himself to the search for forgotten, unknown authors, and no author appearing after the 1990's is included.

🔊 *Lluís Agustí, Instituto Cervantes New York*

Diccionario de bibliología y ciencias afines: terminología relativa a archivística, artes e industrias gráficas, bibliofilia, bibliografía, bibliología, bibliotecología. *(Dictionary of Bibliology and Related Sciences: Terminilogy Relative Archives and Cataloguing, Graphic Arts and Industries, Bibliphilia, Bibliography, Bibliology and Library Science.)*
Author: José Martínez de Sousa
(Not Translated)

This *Dictionary of Bibliology and Related Sciences* contains more than 14,000 terms, with their equivalents in English and French. Martínez de Sousa is a well-known specialist in bibliology, linguistics and graphic arts, and has produced internationally recognized reference works in those areas: the *Dictionary of Typography and Books*, the *Dictionary of Editing, Typography and Graphic Arts*, and the *Dictionary of Orthography and Orthotypography of Current Spanish Usage*.

🔊 *Lluís Agustí, Instituto Cervantes New York*

Diccionario de dudas y dificultades de la lengua española.
(Dictionary of Spanish Language Usage Doubts and Difficulties)
Author: Manuel Seco
(Not Translated)

As its title indicates, a dictionary of usage problems has the objective of helping the speaker resolve quandaries relative to both speech and writing in those aspects of the language where there is uncertainty concerning forms and usage. Language scholar Manuel Seco is a figure of renown in the field of lexicography and this dictionary is a classic which has undergone numerous editions in response to new challenges presented by a linguistic reality in constant evolution.
Lluís Agustí, Instituto Cervantes New York

Diccionario de escritores en lengua castellana: quién es quién hoy en las letras españolas. *(Dictionary of Spanish Language Writers: Who's Who in Spanish Letters Today.)*
Author: Twiggy Hirota, ed.
(Not Translated)

An updated edition of Balay BE1458/Walford7 3:#8298, the 1988 edition having slipped through the cracks. Now limited to writers in Castilian. Entries indicate place and year of birth, present position with an occasional address, published works, anthologies, and prizes. No index.
Jeffry Larson, Yale University Library

Diccionario de hombres y mujeres ilustres de Puerto Rico y de hechos históricos. *(Dictionary of Illustrious Men, Women and Historical Events of Puerto Rico)*
Author: Vicente Reynal
(Not Translated)

Reynal offers an illustrated list of notable people from colonial times to the recent past. Contains a brief section on historical facts and a section illustrating Puerto Rican national symbols.
Nashieli Marcano, University of Akron

REFERENCE ●

Diccionario de la lengua española. *(Dictionary of the Spanish Language)*
Author: Real Academia Española
(Not Translated)

The dictionary of the Royal Academy of Spanish Languaje, commonly known by its Spanish acronym DRAE, is undoubtedly the official dictionary of the Spanish language, and is accepted as such by a great majority of Spanish speakers.
🔊 *Paloma Celis Carbajal, UW-Madison*

Diccionario de la literatura española e hispanoamericana.
(Dictionary of Spanish and Hispanic-American Literature)
Author: Ricardo Gullón, dir.
(Not Translated)

An excellent dictionary of authors, themes and movements of Spanish and Hispanic-American literatures of all times. A key reference work due to its informational value and quality. The entries are signed and include a brief bibliography at the end.
🔊 *Lluís Agustí, Instituto Cervantes New York*

Diccionario de la música española e hispanoamericana.
(Dictionary of Spanish and Hispanic-American Music)
Author: Emilio Casares Rodicio, dir. and general coord., José López-Calo, and Ismael Fernández de la Cuesta, dirs.
(Not Translated)

A comprehensive reference work about music in Spain and Hispanic-American countries. Contains more than 24,000 entries which cover the history, characteristics, relationships, resources and protagonists of Spanish and Hispanic-American musical culture. Includes biographies of composers, singers, dancers, musicologists, teachers, librettists, instrument makers, music critics and promoters, set designers, editors and printers, writers, choreographers, philosophers, scientists and businessmen connected to the music world. This work was sponsored by General Association of Authors and Editors (SGAE) and by the National Institute of Theatrical Arts and Music (INAEM), a dependency of Spain's Ministry of Education, Culture and Sports.
🔊 *Lluís Agustí, Instituto Cervantes New York*

Diccionario de símbolos. *(A Dictionary of Symbols)*
Author: Juan Eduardo Cirlot
(Translated)

Cirlot's *Dictionary of Symbols* is a great reference source for students in the humanities or arts. The illustrations are a useful orientation to elucidate the meanings of the symbols.
🦟 *Yara Larie Cruz, Universal Career Community College*

Diccionario del cine español. *(Dictionary of Spanish Film)*
Author: José Luis Borau, ed.
(Not Translated)

This dictionary was sponsored and endorsed by the Academy of Cinematographic Arts and Sciences of Spain. It contains approximately 1,400 entries arranged alphabetically with information about directors, actors, producers, screen writers, film festivals, production houses, etc. It includes a terminal index for more than 5,000 film titles with references to the entry or entries for the articles in which they are cited.
🦟 *Lluís Agustí, Instituto Cervantes New York*

Diccionario del Quijote: la obra para entender uno de los libros esenciales de la cultura universal. *(A Don Quixote Dictionary: The Book You Need to Understand One of the Essential Works of Universal Culture)*
Author: César Vidal
(Not Translated)

After a 131-page introduction that sets the novel in its context, this semi-scholarly dictionary covers the terms, characters, and themes in Cervantes' masterpiece. Omits mention of Howard Mancing's *Cervantes Encyclopedia* (see Choice, Sept. 2004). Includes cross-references and a 68-page bibliography; no index.
🦟 *Jeffry Larson, Yale University Library*

Diccionario del uso del español. *(Dictionary of Spanish Usage)*
Author: María Moliner
(Not Translated)

Extraordinary reference work for readers interested in more than just one simple definition of a word. In the words of its author, this work was conceived as a guide to Spanish usage for both native speakers and those students who have reached that point in their knowledge where a dictionary in the language being learned should be substituted for the bilingual dictionary. And so, firstly, it provides the user with all the resources available in the language needed to name a thing, to express an idea with maximum precision, or to realize verbally any expressive act. And secondly, it resolves the user's doubts about the legitimacy or illegitimacy of an expression, about the correct way to resolve a certain construction, and so on.

🔊 *Paloma Celis Carbajal, UW-Madison*

Diccionario del verbo español, hispanoamericano y dialectal.
(Dictionary of Spanish, Hispanic-American and Dialectal Verbs)
Author: Jaime Suances-Torres
(Not Translated)

Conjugations, etymologies, definitions and specific usages of countries and regions. Regular, semi-regular, and irregular conjugations. A must have reference book.

🔊 *Lluís Agustí, Instituto Cervantes New York*

Diccionario fraseológico documentado del español actual: locuciones y modismos. *(Dictionary of Documented Phraseology of Modern Spanish: Phrases and Idioms)*
Author: Manuel Seco
(Not Translated)

A scholarly dictionary of Spanish phrases and locutions based on the author's general *Diccionario del españôl actual* (1999), noted in our Fall 2000 issue. Entries indicate variants, grammatical categories, level and area of usage, as well as sourced illustrative citations. Includes a 22-page bibliography of cited texts.

🔊 *Jeffry Larson, Yale University Library*

Diccionario ideológico de la lengua española.
(Ideological Dictionary of the Spanish Language)
Author: Julio Casares
(Not Translated)

Julio Casares' lexicographical work is a great aid for writing clearly and richly, and for finding the exact words which sometimes escape us. This dictionary includes, besides the alphabetic entries common to any dictionary, and ideological classification of words, to proceed, as the author says, «from the idea to the word; from the word to the idea». Words are presented organized by analogy, by semantic relationships and by families of ideas. Equally useful for writers, translators or person who wish to express themselves with precision, relevance and clarity.

🔊 *Lluís Agustí, Instituto Cervantes New York*

Diccionario panhispánico de dudas.
(The PanHispanic Dictionary of Usage Doubts)
Author: Real Academia Española
(Not Translated)

Twenty-two academies of the Spanish language collaborated for five years in the making of this dictionary, a tool whose objective is to resolve questions related to Spanish usage across the entire community of Spanish speakers.
🔍 *Paloma Celis Carbajal, UW-Madison*

Enciclopedia de la novela española. *(Encyclopedia of the Spanish Novel)*
Author: Rafael del Moral
(Not Translated)

In the manner of Porto Bompiani historic literary dictionary, Rafael del Moral includes a selection of more than 700 Spanish novels, each of which is given a brief reference about the subject and intention of the author, a summary of the plot, a brief textual analysis of the novel's style and characters, a critic's appreciation and its connection to other works. A complementary bibliography follows each entry. The objective of the work is not critical appraisal, but rather to provide orientation to professors and students, to help readers decide on new reading, or as a mnemonic aid to remember specifics about readings. And of course, it can't be avoided, it also helps students who have not read the book with their task.
🔍 *Lluís Agustí, Instituto Cervantes New York*

Enciclopedia Hispánica. *(The Hispanic Encyclopedia)*
Author: Encyclopaedia Britannica
(Not Translated)

The *Enciclopedia Hispánica* is one of the most authoritative, up-to-date, and comprehensive encyclopedia published in Spanish.
🔍 *Alvaro Sanabria, San Francisco Public Library*

Encyclopedia Latina: History, Culture and Society in the United States.
Author: Ilan Stavans, editor in chief, and Harold Augenbraum, associate editor
(In English)

In spite of its alphabetical order, this reference work is more precisely a thematic encyclopedia, with emphasis on aspects of the culture, society, language and art of Latinos in the United States. The work is not exempt from the controversy often provoked by the work of Ilan Stavans, see, for example, the entry for Spanglish. Each entry is followed by cross-references and a complementary bibliography.
🔍 *Lluís Agustí, Instituto Cervantes New York*

Encyclopedia of Contemporary Latin American and Caribbean Cultures.
Author: Daniel Balderston, Mike Gonzalez, and Ana M. López, eds.
(In English)

The *Encyclopedia of Contemporary Latin American and Caribbean Cultures* contains more than 4,000 brief entries in English about society, politics and culture after 1920 in said regions. A quick reference tool, ideal for obtaining abstracts about any subject relative to the contemporary Latin American situation.
🔊 *Lluís Agustí, Instituto Cervantes New York*

Encyclopedia of Contemporary Spanish Culture.
Author: Eamonn Rodgers, ed.
(In English)

Thematic encyclopedia about society, culture, history, art, and politics in Spain from the end of the Civil War until the present. Written in English, it contains more than 700 entries in alphabetical order. Each entry is followed by references, as well as by a complementary bibliography.
🔊 *Lluís Agustí, Instituto Cervantes New York*

Encyclopedia of Latin American History and Culture.
Author: Barbara A. Tenembaum, and Georgette M. Dorn, eds.
(In English)

A classic reference work in English compiled by specialists of wide acclaim, this five volume works includes more than 5,300 entries in alphabetical order about countries, institutions and persons. A brief bibliography at the end of each entry complements the information.
🔊 *Lluís Agustí, Instituto Cervantes New York*

El español en el mundo: anuario del Instituto Cervantes.
(Spanish in the World: Yearbook of the Cervantes Institute)
Author: Instituto Cervantes
(Not Translated)

Spanish in the World is the general title of the yearbooks which, since 1998, have been published by the Cervantes Institute. These works, written with a merely descriptive purpose, propose to complete a minute examination of the extent and the importance of Spanish usage and cover subjects of lasting interest.
🔊 *Salvador Vergara, Instituto Cervantes Chicago*

Evas terrenales: biobibliografías de 150 autoras dominicanas.
(Earthly Eves: Biographies and Bibliographys of 150 Dominican Women Writers)
Author: Franklin Gutiérrez
(Not Translated)

This unique volume in the literary bibliography genre of the island, comprehensively describes the works of over 150 female Dominican writers. Over 3,000 passive and active bibliographical entries make this text a must-read for those analyzing the contribution of the Dominican women to the literary formation of the country.
🔖 *Nashieli Marcano, University of Akron*

The Firefly Spanish/English Visual Dictionary.
Author: Jean-Claude Corbeil, and Ariane Archambault
(Bilingual)

This bilingual pictorial dictionary is an extraordinary tool, which identifies more than 25,000 terms by means of thousands of detailed and precise illustrations. It is organized by topic: astronomy, geography, animal kingdom, plant kingdom, the human being, agriculture, architecture, homes, household items, gardening, home repair, dress, personal accoutrements, communications, transportation. Includes entries like the parts of a faucet in Spanish and their English equivalents, the instruments in an orchestra, the different parts of a sailboat, in short, the names of the reality in which we live, often difficult to describe solely by the words of a regular dictionary.
🔖 *Lluís Agustí, Instituto Cervantes New York*

Gramática de la lengua castellana dedicada al uso de los americanos.
(A Grammar of the Castilian Language for Use by Hispanic Americans)
Author: Andrés Bello
(Non Translated)

This work is not only considered to be the best reference grammar in the Castilian language, but also one of the best ever written in any language.
🔖 *Marlenys Villamar, Professor*

Gramática descriptiva de la lengua española.
(Descriptive Grammar of the Spanish Language)
Author: Ignacio Bosque, and Violeta Demonte, dirs.
(Not Translated)

This reference work covers among other subjects: the basic syntax of word types, fundamental syntactical constructions, temporal, aspectual, and model relationships, sentences and speech, and lexical morphology.
🔖 *Lluís Agustí, Instituto Cervantes New York*

Gran diccionario Oxford: español-inglés, inglés-español = The Oxford Spanish Dictionary: Spanish-English, English-Spanish.
Author: Beatriz Galimberti Jarman, and Roy Russell
(Bilingual)

One of the most extensive and complete bilingual dictionaries of the Spanish and English languages. A dictionary of current usage, it contains more than 300,000 words and phrases, and also includes grammatical charts, verb conjugations, examples of private and business correspondence, résumés in both languages, examples of email usage and SMS.

 Lluís Agustí, Instituto Cervantes New York

Gran enciclopedia cervantina, v. 1: A buen bocado, buen grito.
(Great Cervantean Encyclopedia, Vol. 1: «Good to the Taste, Mouth Open in Haste»)
Author: Carlos Alvar, dir.
(Not Translated)

An ambitious encyclopedia to be complete in 10 volumes covering all aspects of Cervantes, his work, and his world and legacy, with the publisher claiming at least 120 international scholars authoring 25,000 entries. The signed entries include occasional tables of contents for longer articles, illustrative quotations from Cervantes' works with appropriate, selected bibliography, and cross-references. No mention found of any index or illustrations.

 Jeffry Larson, Yale University Library

Gran enciclopedia de España. *(Great Encyclopedia of Spain)*
Author: Guillermo Fatás Cabeza, dir.
(Not Translated)

This alphabetic encyclopedia in 22 volumes focuses exclusively on Spain, covering geography, population, history, art, economy, culture and comprehensive information about all the autonomous communities, provinces, and municipalities of the country. Recently completed, the last volume has just been published. An indispensable work for libraries which require precise and up-to-date information about Spain.

Lluís Agustí, Instituto Cervantes New York

La guerra civil española: fuentes (archivos, bibliografía y filmografía).
(The Spanish Civil War: Sources (Archives, Bibliography, Filmography))
Author: Juan García Durán
(Not Translated)

This reference work is indispensable for anyone researching the Spanish Civil War, in or outside in Spain. It compiles all primary and secondary sources of informative relative to the conflict, including military, political and social perspectives.
🔍 *Lluís Agustí, Instituto Cervantes New York*

Historia de la literatura española. *(History of Spanish Literature)*
Author: Juan Luis Alborg
(Not Translated)

A history of literature in Spanish, organized chronologically by periods, themes and authors. Chapters on Medieval, Renaissance, Baroque, 18th century, 19th century and contemporary literature. Although first published more than 40 years ago in 1966, Alborg's work, in its second and extended edition of 1970, continues to be an indispensable reference.
🔍 *Lluís Agustí, Instituto Cervantes New York*

Historia de las mujeres en España y América Latina.
(History of Women in Spain and Latin America)
Author: Isabel Morant, dir.
(Not Translated)

This is a history of women from prehistoric times to the present day. Comprising 4 volumes with contributions from more than 30 specialists, it constitutes an essential guide for all those who wish to explore the situation, condition, position, conduct and reality of women throughout history in Spain and Latin America. It contains, besides an index of names, an extensive bibliography about the periods and subjects covered.
🔍 *Salvador Vergara, Instituto Cervantes Chicago*

Historia documental del cine mexicano.
(Documentary History of the Mexican Cinema)
Author: Emilio García Riera
(Not Translated)

The history of Mexican cinema, one of the best and most important examples of the art in the Spanish language, can count on the most extensive and detailed study undertaken to date about any Hispanic cinematographic tradition. Chronologically and throughout its 18 volumes, Emilio García Riera covers each era by dissecting each and every production therein. This is an indispensable work for any library specializing in Hispanic studies.

🔊 *Lluís Agustí, Instituto Cervantes New York*

Historia general de las artes plásticas en Puerto Rico.
(General History of the Plastic Arts in Puerto Rico)
Author: Osiris Delgado Mercado
(Not Translated)

This work surveys many aspects of the arts in Puerto Rico. Each chapter includes an extensive essay with supplemental notes, many illustrations, appendices, and a bibliography. A name and geographical index provides further access.

🔊 *Nashieli Marcano, University of Akron*

Historia y crítica de la literatura española.
(Spanish Literature: History and Criticism)
Author: Francisco Rico, ed.
(Not Translated)

A few years ago language professor Francisco Rico began this magnificent work which over time has become a mandatory reference for the history of peninsular Spanish literature. It systematically compiles the best contributions of contemporary critics about every historical period of Spanish literature, including themes, names and works.

🔊 *Lluís Agustí, Instituto Cervantes New York*

Historia y crítica de la literatura hispanoamericana.
(Hispanic-American Literature: History and Criticism)
Author: Cedomil Goic, ed.
(Not Translated)

Paralleling the work of Francisco Rico, *History and Criticism of Spanish Literature*, about peninsular Spanish literature, the work of Cedomil Goic compiles the best contributions of contemporary critics about all the historical periods of Hispanic-American literature, including themes, names and works.

🔊 *Lluís Agustí, Instituto Cervantes New York*

Los instrumentos de la música afrocubana. *(Afro-Cuban Musical Instruments)*
Author: Fernando Ortiz
(Not Translated)

Perhaps the most exhaustive study effected by an individual about Afro-Cuban music, its instruments and its history. The author, Fernando Ortiz, an academic of encyclopedic knowledge, wrote about popular religion and speech, and about Cuban culture in general. This is indispensable reference work about the music of the Caribbean.

🔍 *Pedro Canó, Instituto Cervantes New York*

Latin American Studies: An Annotated Bibliography of Core Works.
Author: Ana María Cobos, and Ana Lya Sater
(In English)

Compiled by librarians, this bibliography in English about Latin American studies contains 1,400 recent bibliographical recommendations. Organized thematically and geographically, this is a very useful tool for librarians and researchers.

🔍 *Lluís Agustí, Instituto Cervantes New York*

Literatura centroamericana: diccionario de autores centroamericanos: fuentes para su estudio.
(Central American Literature: Dictionary of Authors and Sources)
Author: Jorge Eduardo Arellano
(Not Translated)

Important reference source that provides brief bio-bibliographic entries for the most recognized Central American fiction writers. The second part «Fuentes para su estudio» provides up-to-date bibliographies of other reference sources, anthologies, literary surveys, and more.

🔍 *Claude Potts, Arizona State University*

Literatura puertorriqueña: su proceso en el tiempo.
(Puerto Rican Literature: Process Through Time)
Author: Josefina Rivera de Álvarez
(Not Translated)

Rivera de Álvarez's work is the most comprehensive reference text on Puerto Rican literature to date. From Pre-Columbian mythology, to literary works of the 30's, 40's and 60's, the text incorporates extensive notes that include references to secondary literature, as well as a lengthy bibliography.

🔍 *Nashieli Marcano, University of Akron*

Manual del librero hispanoamericano. *(Manual of the Hispanic-American Bookseller)*
Author: Antonio Palau y Dulcet
(Not Translated)

Commonly called the Palau Manual, a work of a single person, secondhand bookseller Antonio Palau y Dulcet, this is undoubtedly the best bibliography of Spanish and Hispanic-American editions of all time. Compiles publications from the invention of printing to the 20th century. Useful for librarians, scholars, secondhand and antiquarian booksellers, and collectors.
 Lluís Agustí, Instituto Cervantes New York

El mercado del libro antiguo español: una guía de precios.
(The Spanish Rare Books Market: A Pricing Guide)
Author: Julio Ollero, and Susana Bardón, eds.
(Not Translated)

This is a reference work providing guidance for private individuals, booksellers and librarians who at some point may be confronted with the need to monetarily assess tomes in Spanish of great age. The work compiles more than 14,000 entries for books (from incunabula until 1850) and their prices, obtained from booksellers' catalogues. Without having the informative nor organizational richness of the *Manual of the Hispanic-American Bookseller* by Antonio Palau y Dulcet, it nonetheless helps to clarify many doubts. The work was subsequently expanded in a second volume which covers references to more modern books: *From the Generation of '98 to the Literature of the 1960's: A Pricing Guide.*
 Lluís Agustí, Instituto Cervantes New York

Mujeres novelistas y novelas de mujeres en la posguerra española (1940-1965).
(Women Novelists and Novels by Women in Post War Spain (1940-1965))
Author: Raquel Conde Pen Alosa
(Not Translated)

A selective catalog of serious adult novels written by Spanish women in Castilian in the mid-20th century, excluding (most) short stories, genre fiction, and young adult and children's literature. Entries indicate first and successive editions, translations and adaptations, a genre or thematic label, prizes won, brief synopsis, and stylistic commentary. Includes indexes of works, chronology, and genres/themes, as well as rankings by number of reprints and prizes won. Also includes brief author biographies and a 21-page bibliography.
Jeffry Larson, Yale University Library

Nueva enciclopedia de Puerto Rico. *(New Encyclopedia of Puerto Rico)*
Author: José A. Toro-Sugrañés
(Not Translated)

This reference work is a compilation of over 30 years of research, studies and experiences of its contributors. It provides students with a comprehensive source in the fields of geography, history, culture and ecology.
🔒 *Nashieli Marcano, University of Akron*

Ortografía de la lengua española. Edición revisada por las Academias de la Lengua Española. *(Orthography of the Spanish Language)*
Author: Real Academia Española
(Not Translated)

A useful, clear and indispensable tool in reference to doubts about Spanish usage and style, covering when and how to use capital letters, abbreviations, place names, etc., explained in a precise and relevant way with clear and illustrative examples. The current has been revised by the Academies of the Spanish Language, which is to say, its contents are of common accord with all variants of Spanish in the Americas.
🔒 *Lluís Agustí, Instituto Cervantes New York*

Ortografía y ortotipografía del español actual.
(Orthography and Orthotypography of Modern Spanish)
Author: José Martínez de Sousa
(Not Translated)

An essential book for every translator and a great aid with everything having to do with the editing of texts.
🔒 *Marko Miletich, Binghamton University (SUNY)*

Plan curricular del Instituto Cervantes: niveles de referencia para el español.
(Instituto Cervantes Curriculum Program: Reference Levels for Spanish)
Author: Instituto Cervantes
(Not Translated)

Instituto Cervantes is the Spanish government institution devoted to promoting and disseminating the Spanish language. This great work grows out of the practical application of official European theories on language teaching, in this case applied to Spanish. The four volumes describe and analyze linguistic resources for preparing and achieving the objectives and content of programs for teaching Spanish as a foreign language. An essential reference work for teachers and educational administrators.

🔊 *Lluís Agustí, Instituto Cervantes New York*

Puerto Rico la gran cocina del Caribe.
(Puerto Rico: The Great Caribbean Cuisine)
Author: José Díaz de Villegas
(Not Translated)

An excellent cookbook. Incorporates typical ingredients of local Caribbean cuisine to create both new and traditional recipes.

🔊 *Yara Larie Cruz, Universal Career Community College*

Puerto Rico, cinco siglos de historia.
(Puerto Rico: Five Centuries of History)
Author: Francisco Scarano
(Not Translated)

This is one of the best books about the history of Puerto Rico, used in teaching the history of the island from the pre-colonial era to modern times.

🔊 *Yara Larie Cruz, Universal Career Community College*

Redes: diccionario combinatorio del español contemporáneo.
(Webs: A Combinatorial Dictionary of Contemporary Spanish)
Author: Ignacio de Bosque, dir.
(Not Translated)

«I am myself and my circumstance» was a celebrated phrase of Spanish philosopher José Ortega y Gasset. This innovative dictionary proposes something similar. Strangely titled *Webs: A Different Lexicographic Organizing Principle* (*Redes: una organización lexicográfica distinta*), it proceeds from the notion that words do not have any intrinsic meaning, but rather only when combined with each other, in other words, with accompanying or surrounding words. Directed by language scholar Ignacio Bosque, this dictionary does not define words, but rather shows combinations of words relative to their meaning. The dictionary was created based on texts from 68 publications from Spanish and American presses during the last 20 years, or more than 250 million words.

🔊 *Lluís Agustí, Instituto Cervantes New York*

Teatro español: (de la A a la Z). *(The Spanish Theatre from A to Z)*
Author: Javier Huerta Calvo, Emilio Peral Vega, and Héctor Urzáiz Tortajada
(Not Translated)

A scholarly encyclopedia of theater of all periods in all the languages (80% Castilian) of Spain. Covers playwrights, selected plays, theatrical concepts, directors and other theater professionals; articles give biographical sketches, lists of major works, and references to the 20-page end bibliography. Also includes lists of entries treating works and terms, cross-references, and an index of works treated.
🔖 *Jeffry Larson, Yale University Library*

El universo de las lenguas: clasificación, denominación, situación, tipología, historia y bibliografía de las lenguas.
(The Language Universe: Classification, Denomination, Categorization, Typology, History and Bibliography of Languages)
Author: Juan Carlos Moreno Cabrera
(Not Translated)

This is a key reference work which provides, in orderly and systematic fashion, information about the classification, genetic affiliation, geo-demographic situation, type of grammatical structure, and history of all languages.
🔖 *Salvador Vergara, Instituto Cervantes Chicago*

CHILDREN
YOUNG ADULTS

ABC de Puerto Rico. *(A Puerto Rican ABC)*
Author: Paola Nogueras
(Not Translated)

Youngsters will be able to practice the alphabet while they learn about Puerto Rican culture and the island landscape. Adults will enjoy the impressive photography.
🔖 *Sabrina Abreu, Instituto Cervantes New York*

Antes de ser libres. *(Before We Were Free)*
Author: Julia Álvarez
(Translated)

At twelve years of age, Anita de la Torre does not understand the tensions which move the political life of her country, although each day she witnesses the disappearance from her world of another member of her family, her neighborhood or her school. Against the background of the Trujillo dictatorship in the Dominican Republic, Julia Álvarez makes us feel the fear and the innocence, the injustice and the force of power experienced by the de la Torre family, who in the end must follow the path taken by so many Dominicans and abandon the only life they've ever known.
🔖 *F. Isabel Campoy, Transformative Education*

Ay, luna, luna, lunita... *(Oh, Moon, Lune, Demilune!)*
Author: Yanitzia Canetti, and Ángeles Peinador, il.
(Not Translated)

A playful tale of repetitions with an astonishing ending which will both amuse and amaze readers.
🔖 *Georgina Lázaro, Writer*

¡Azúcar! *(Groove!)*
Author: Ivar Da Coll
(Not Translated)

This biography, written and illustrated with children in mind, details the life of Celia Cruz, the Queen of Salsa. From her birth in Havana, Cuba, to her funeral in Miami, author/illustrator Ivar Da Coll uses poetry and humor to describe the important milestones in the star's life, and captures the true essence of her colorful, vibrant personality. The vivid illustrations bring this real-life fairy tale to life.
🔖 *Teresa Mlawer, Lectorum Publications Inc.*

Bajo las palmas reales: una infancia cubana.
(Under the Royal Palms. A Childhood in Cuba)
Author: Alma Flor Ada
(Translated)

This version in Spanish of *Under the Royal Palms. A Childhood in Cuba*, winner of the American Library Association's Pura Belpre Prize in 2000, has been published by Alfaguara. Various chapters of the book, each one a vignette of a moment in the childhood of the author, have been included in many textbooks in the United States, both in English and in Spanish, in the areas of Reading, Language Arts and Social Studies, as a model of the ability to observe the reality which surrounds us in life and to find profound meaning in each moment. The book has gone through numerous editions and its author receives voluminous correspondence from teachers and students who have felt inspired to write the stories of their own lives, based on their reading of this book.
🔊 *F. Isabel Campoy, Transformative Education*

Una biblioteca para Juana: el mundo de Sor Juana Inés.
(A Library for Juana: the World of Sor Juana Inés)
Author: Pat Mora
(Translated)

Juana Ramírez de Asbaje is a girl inspired by learning, and since the age of three has insisted that she be allowed to learn to read. That passion never leaves her and thus she convinces her family to send her to Mexico City, governed at the time by a Spanish viceroy. To quench her thirst for the knowledge contained in books, she enters a convent and there becomes the first great poet of Latin America. Although this biography of Sister Juana Inés de la Cruz is intended for children and only covers part of this woman's exceptional life (it does not recount the terrible price she paid for her intelligence), Pat Mora nonetheless is able to convey the tenacity, intelligence and courage of this great 17th century woman writer.
🔊 *F. Isabel Campoy, Transformative Education*

La cazadora de Indiana Jones. *(Indiana Jones's Jacket)*
Author: Asun Balzola
(Not Translated)

Christie's family is without means and she's forced to wear her brother's hand-me-downs, including his jacket. To avoid teasing by her friends and classmates, Christie tells them the jacket belonged to Indiana Jones.
🔊 *Lluís Agustí, Instituto Cervantes New York*

La ciudad y las bestias. *(City of the Beasts)*
Author: Isabel Allende
(Translated)

In Isabel Allende's first novel for young readers, Alexander Cold sets off on an Amazonian expedition with his grandmother in search of «the Beast», a Yeti-like creature. Along the way he learns a great deal about other cultures, the importance of nature, and himself.
🐾 *Teresa Mlawer, Lectorum Publications Inc.*

Colibrí. *(Colibrí)*
Author: Ann Cameron
(Translated)

Twelve-year-old Rosa hardly remembers the home she shared with her loving parents before she was kidnapped at the age of four. Since then, she has traveled with Uncle, an abusive con artist, who has been convinced by a fortune-teller that Rosa will make him rich. As she is forced to lie and beg for money, a compelling, suspenseful story unfolds.
🐾 *Teresa Mlawer, Lectorum Publications Inc.*

Completamente diferente. *(Completely Different)*
Author: Yanitzia Canetti, and Ángeles Peinador, il.
(Not Translated)

A lovely blue hippopotamus is the protagonist of this picture book that deals with important topics such as tolerance, segregation, and discrimination. Bombolina wants to make friends, but the other animals find her too different and prefer to keep to their own kind. Finally, a tiny yellow fish points out that it is better to focus on what they have in common, and the two become friends.
🐾 *Teresa Mlawer, Lectorum Publications Inc.*

Cosas que pasan. *(Things Happen)*
Author: Isol
(Not Translated)

The little girl in this story would gallop to school if she only had a horse. She would be stronger, prettier, and taller if she had any say in it. When a genie appears and agrees to grant her one wish, she must decide which one to choose.
🐾 *Teresa Mlawer, Lectorum Publications Inc.*

Cuéntame un cuento. *(Tell Me a Story)*
Author: Concha Cardenoso
(Not Translated)

This book compiles famous fables, such as *Beauty and the Beast, Cinderella, The Match Seller, The Emperor's New Clothes, The Princess and the Pea, Raposo and the Fishmongers,* etc.

🔊 *Guillermina Raffo Magnasco, St Thomas University*

Cuentos al amor de la lumbre. *(Stories in the Light of Love)*
Author: Antonio Rodríguez Almodóvar
(Not Translated)

These stories collected by Rodríguez Almodóvar all have provenance in the traditional cultural heritage of Spain. The author carried out extensive research and collected in a scientific and systematic way, but also with a literary talent for adaptation, this anthology of popular Spanish stories which has become through its various editions a mandatory reference work for those seeking to learn about the storytelling tradition in Spain.

🔊 *Lluís Agustí, Instituto Cervantes New York*

Cuentos de la selva. *(Jungle Tales for Children)*
Author: Horacio Quiroga
(Translated)

A must for any children.

🔊 *Daniel Berdaner, Dallas Public Library*

Cuentos del fondo del mar. *(Stories from the Bottom of the Sea)*
Author: Silvia Dubovoy, and Ángeles Peinador, il.
(Not Translated)

Sharks, squids, turtles, penguins, and lobsters are just some of the characters that inhabit the pages of this book of wonderful marine stories. Written by an expert in the field, these tales bring to vivid life an amazing underwater world.

🔊 *Teresa Mlawer, Lectorum Publications Inc.*

Cuentos para chicos y grandes. *(Stories for the Young and Old)*
Author: Hilda Perera, and Rapi Diego, il.
(Not Translated)

This exceptional collection of exquisitely written short stories will surely tug at the heartstrings of readers of all ages.These stories, which earned the author Spain's most prestigious children's literature award, touch upon universal themes such as hope, love, freedom, and truth.
🔊 *Teresa Mlawer, Lectorum Publications Inc.*

Cuentos que contaban nuestras abuelas.
(Tales Our Abuelitas Told: A Hispanic Folktale Collection)
Author: F. Isabel Campoy, and Alma Flor Ada
(Translated)

A mixture of popular tales and literary lore, this anthology celebrates Hispanic culture and its many roots —Indigenous, African, Arab, Hebrew, and Spanish. Four leading Latino artists brilliantly illustrate the twelve stories in this collection, which embody the lively spirit and the rich heritage of Latino people.
🔊 *Teresa Mlawer, Lectorum Publications Inc.*

El día de muertos. *(The Day of the Dead)*
Author: Ivar Da Coll
(Not Translated)

Every year, on November 2nd, Grandma comes and teaches all about the Day of the Dead. Through her stories, we learn the importance of this Mexican holiday, and about the traditions that make the day special, from making altars for our deceased loved ones to baking treats in the shape of skeletons. Humorous, colorful illustrations add the perfect touch to this truly original book of verse.
🔊 *Teresa Mlawer, Lectorum Publications Inc.*

Doña Piñones. *(Doña Piñones)*
Author: María de la Luz Uribe
(Not Translated)

An amusing and funny story written in rhyme which will prove enchanting to children.
🔊 *Georgina Lázaro, Writer*

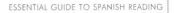

En las cavernas de Camuy: Terón y su maravilloso mundo subterráneo.
(In the Caverns of Camuy: Terón and His Marvelous Underground World)
Author: Wenceslao Serra Deliz
(Not Translated)

The adventures of two kids and a bat unfold when they discover the beauties and wonders of the caverns of Puerto Rico, in particular one of the island's natural reserves: the Caverns of Camuy.
🞐 *Nashieli Marcano, University of Akron*

El enmascarado de lata. *(The Man in the Tin Mask)*
Author: Vivian Mansour Manzur, and Trino, il.
(Not Translated)

With great wit and sensitivity Mexican author Vivian Mansour incorporates the world of Lucha Libre into a little boy's search for self-esteem. The son of *El Enmascarado de Lata* fights for acceptance at school while his dad fights in the ring. It is not until all seems lost that the boy realizes that his dad is a true hero. Famed Mexican caricaturist Trino lends his unique style of artwork to this humorous novel that will appeal to both young and old.
🞐 *Teresa Mlawer, Lectorum Publications Inc.*

Finis mundi. *(Finis mundi)*
Author: Laura Gallego García
(Not Translated)

Michel, a Cluny monk in medieval France, decides to embark on a nearly impossible mission. The end of the world is near and mankind will be doomed unless Michel finds the three axes to invoke the Spirit of Time. However, malevolent forces also want to possess the axes and constantly obstruct Michel's path.
🞐 *Teresa Mlawer, Lectorum Publications Inc.*

El flamboyán amarillo. *(The Yellow Flame Tree)*
Author: Georgina Lázaro, and Lulu Delacre, il.
(Not Translated)

In the new edition of this poetic and captivating story, a boy and his mother find a beautiful flowering tree during their walk through the countryside. The boy decides to take some of that beauty home and picks up a few seeds. When

the tree he planted starts to grow, the boy discovers the miracle of creation. Years later, when the tree finally flowers, there's a marvelous surprise in store. The beautiful illustration vividly recreate the warm Caribbean environment.
🔊 *Teresa Mlawer, Lectorum Publications Inc.*

Fray Perico y su borrico. *(Brother Perico and His Donkey)*
Author: Juan Muñoz Martín
(Not Translated)

A book which cannot be omitted from the reading list of any elementary school child, not only because of the values it espouses, but also because of its literary richness and simplicity.
🔊 *Diego Hernández, Colegio Doral Academy Middle School*

Gathering the Sun: An Alphabet in Spanish and English.
Author: Alma Flor Ada
(Bilingual)

This bilingual alphabet of poems celebrates the dignity of life of migrant farm workers in the United States. With more than 20 editions, it is recognized as a classic of Latin children's literature in the USA. Simón Silva's impressive illustrations, drawn and colored with a firm hand and recalling the great Mexican muralists, contribute to the creation of a whole which celebrates family values, the honor of honest work, the beauty of the fields, and the power of culture. It has received numerous prizes, among which are one from the Simon Wiesenthal Center of the Museum of Tolerance in Los Angeles, the Pura Belpré Honor Book 1997 and a NCSS/CBC Language Arts Notable Book mention.
🔊 *F. Isabel Campoy, Transformative Education*

Las golosinas secretas. *(Secret Treats)*
Author: Juan Villoro, and Mauricio Gómez Morin, il
(Not Translated)

Fito loves his sweets, but not as much as he loves Rosita. When a mean-spirited neighbor uses a magic lipstick to make Rosita disappear, Fito risks everything to rescue her from the world of invisibility. Children will learn the importance of loyalty and friendship through this story.
🔊 *Teresa Mlawer, Lectorum Publications Inc.*

CHILDREN / YOUNG ADULTS ●

Historias de ninguno. *(Stories of Nobody)*
Author: Pilar Mateos
(Not Translated)

This sensitive story is about a little boy so tiny he must put stones in his pockets on a windy day. His classmates nickname him Nobody, and they rarely even notice him. But thanks to a new friendship, Nobody is given the opportunity to experience a series of exciting adventures.
🔍 *Teresa Mlawer, Lectorum Publications Inc.*

Juan Bobo busca trabajo. *(Juan Bobo Goes to Work)*
Author: Marisa Montes, and Joe Cepeda, il.
(Translated)

Juan Bobo (Simple John) is the most famous children's character in Puerto Rico. In spite of his good will and effort in everything he does, nothing comes out right for Juan Bobo. Juan Bobo, mistakes and all, is much loved by all Latin American children.
🔍 *Ramón Caraballo, Bookseller*

Julia. *(Julia)*
Author: Georgina Lázaro, and Poli Marichal, il.
(Not Translated)

Julia tells, in verse, the story of a girl born into a humble Puerto Rican family at the beginning of last century. With beautiful illustrations, it recreates the time in which she grew up, and narrates how she became one of Puerto Rico's and Latin America's most beloved poets. Her name is Julia de Burgos and this is her life before she was big.
🔍 *Teresa Mlawer, Lectorum Publications Inc.*

Juvenilia. *(Juvenilia)*
Author: Miguel Cané
(Translated)

This is a classic book for children. 🔍 *Guillermina Raffo Magnasco, St Thomas University*

Lautaro, joven libertador de Arauco. *(Lautaro)*
Author: Fernando Alegría
(Translated)

Lautaro, the young liberator of Arauco, narrates the history of a young Indian who fights for his people. The history of Spanish conquests are presented in a way which may be understood by young readers.
🔍 *Yara Larie Cruz, Universal Career Community College*

Le comieron la lengua los ratones. *(Cat Got Your Tongue?)*
Author: Silvia Molina, and Mari Rodríguez, il.
(Not Translated)

Presented in verse, this beautifully written story shows how a girl named Mari, who had stopped talking once her mother died, slowly begins to emerge from her grief and live again thanks to a very special uncle, aunt, and group of cousins. Set in Tepexpan, Mexico, this book will appeal to all readers with its message of hope and familial love.
🔸 *Teresa Mlawer, Lectorum Publications Inc.*

La Llorona = The Weeping Woman: An Hispanic Legend Told in Spanish and English.
Author: Joe Hayes
(Bilingual)

The legend of *La Llorona* (The Wheeper) is perhaps one of the most popular legends in all Latin America. This illustrated adaptation relates the story of a beautiful woman, who faced with her husband's rejection, decides to drown her children in the river. A moment later, she realizes the horror of the act, and dies crying and screaming: «My children, my children!» The legend tells that the ghost of this tormented soul sometimes appears searching for her children.
🔸 *Ramón Caraballo, Bookseller*

Mañanario. *(Morning Diary)*
Author: Ricardo Chávez Castañeda
(Not Translated)

Getting over the death of a loved one is very difficult, especially when the person who has died was young and has committed suicide. Written in diary form, this intimate story is harsh and painful, yet it ultimately offers a glimmer of hope. As it reveals the grief that comes with the death of a son and a brother, it also highlights a family's struggle to overcome a dramatic loss.
🔸 *Teresa Mlawer, Lectorum Publications Inc.*

Mi nombre es María Isabel. *(My Name is María Isabel)*
Author: Alma Flor Ada
(Translated)

The story of María Salazar López has been and continues to be that of many Latin children in the United States and the great popularity this book enjoys is due to the author's skill in capturing that reality in a tightly woven plot with a likeable character. When the protagonist arrives at a new school, the teacher decides to call her Mary Lopes. The girl, who strongly identifies with her given names, as she was named after her grandmothers, and with her surnames, which represent her grandfathers, does not recognize herself in that strange appellation. And that leads her to appear inattentive and discourteous, and signals the beginning of ever more complicated problems. There have been numerous editions of this book; indeed, it is among the best-selling books of all times by a Latin author in the U.S. Recognized as a Notable Book by the National Social Studies Association and the National Association of Language Arts, it has been included in the prestigious anthology of the best children's literature written in the English language, the Norton Children's Literature Anthology.

🔍 *F. Isabel Campoy, Transformative Education*

Miguel Vicente pata caliente. *(Miguel Vicente Puts the Pedal to the Metal)*
Author: Orlando Araujo
(Not Translated)

Miguel Vicente, a shoeshine boy who lives in a Caracas slum, dreams of traveling to faraway places. When he is given a book about Marco Polo, it sparks his imagination and he joins his brother —a truck driver— on a journey through Venezuela.

🔍 *Teresa Mlawer, Lectorum Publications Inc.*

La moneda de oro. *(The Gold Coin)*
Author: Alma Flor Ada, and Neil Waldman, il.
(Translated)

Juan knows that the old woman Josefa has a treasure, a gold coin, and he's determined to steal it, even though to do so he must pursue her to the ends of the earth. While in pursuit he realizes the labor of love done by the likable old woman and the compassion she feels for the least fortunate.

🔍 *Ramón Caraballo, Bookseller*

Negrita. *(Negrita)*
Author: Onelio Jorge Cardoso
(Not Translated)

The history of a long and deep friendship between a peasant and his dog, Negrita. Readers will be moved by the beautiful writing which speaks to us of such important themes as liberty and equality.

🔍 *Teresa Mlawer, Lectorum Publications, Inc.*

El niño que conversaba con la mar. *(The Boy Who Talked to the Sea)*
Author: Enrique Pérez Díaz
(Not Translated)

In this touching story by a Cuban author, a little boy who lives by the sea sails a paper boat every day on his way to school. In this way, he hopes to communicate with the people he misses, especially his father, who left one stormy night on a raft he made from an old truck tire.
🔊 *Teresa Mlawer, Lectorum Publications Inc.*

El palacio de la medianoche. *(Midnight Palace)*
Author: Carlos Ruiz Zafón
(Not Translated)

The intricate plot of this page-turner revolves around an orphanage in India, a baby left in its care, and the forces of both friendship and evil. When the child, dubbed Ben, grows up and is about to strike out on his own, he is confronted with the past he never knew. Both he and his friends are in for the adventure of their lives when they enter into a world of the supernatural in search of clues about Ben's father.
🔊 *Teresa Mlawer, Lectorum Publications Inc.*

Paula en Nueva York. *(Paula in New York)*
Author: Mikel Valverde
(Not Translated)

Fun story about a fantastic voyage and the curious stay of a girl in New York City.
🔊 *Georgina Lázaro, Writer*

Pedrín y la garza. *(Pedrín and the Stork)*
Author: Hilda Perera, and Enrique Sánchez Moreiro, il.
(Not Translated)

Taken from the award-winning book of short stories, *Stories for Youngsters and Adults* (*Cuentos para chicos y grandes*), comes this illustrated tale of a lonely boy named Pedrín, who nurses a wounded stork back to health. Although he loves the bird, he understands its desire to be free and rejoices as it flies through the sky. The artwork, a mixture of photographs and illustrations, adds a very realistic touch to the book's moving message which will touch the hearts of all.
🔊 *Teresa Mlawer, Lectorum Publications Inc.*

El peinado de la tía Chofi. *(Aunt Chofi's Hairdo)*
Author: Vivian Mansour Manzur, and Martha Avilés, il.
(Not Translated)

This hilarious, uproarious, endearing story tells of a little tiny beetle that takes refuge in Tía Chofi's six-foot tall hairdo on the way to a wedding. The chaos that ensues teaches Tía Chofi that a hat might be the best hairdo after all.
🔊 *Teresa Mlawer, Lectorum Publications Inc.*

La peineta colorada. *(The Red Comb)*
Author: Fernando Picó
(Translated)

Filled with Puerto Rican colloquial language and based on historical facts, Picó's text tells the story of how a young girl and her grandmother help a runaway slave. In a compelling fashion, this story captures the interest of readers, enabling them to engage in constructive dialogues.
🔊 *Nashieli Marcano, University of Akron*

Perdido. *(Lost)*
Author: Hilda Perera
(Not Translated)

«It's true than once I bit my owner, I didn't like him that much: we both wanted to command. From being a dog come the biting and barking and attacking when attacked; from being a brave and fierce dog; and I can't fly or be a pigeon, because each one is what he is. I'm sorry, owner, but I live and act as I am. I was born a dog. Don't ask for miracles.»
🔊 *Teresa Mlawer, Lectorum Publications Inc.*

Platero y Juan Ramón. *(Platero and Juan Ramón)*
Author: Carlos Reviejo, and Ulises Wensell, il.
(Not Translated)

This book provides a fun way to introduce young children to Juan Ramón Jiménez and his classic *Platero and I* (*Platero y yo*). A pictorial vocabulary key to all the substituted words appears at the back of the book.
🔊 *Teresa Mlawer, Lectorum Publications Inc.*

Pocopán. *(Short Stories)*
Author: María Elena Walsh
(Translated)

This is a famous book with interesting stories that encourage critical thinking on the children.
🔍 *Guillermina Raffo Magnasco, St Thomas University*

El polizón del Ulises. *(Ulysses's Stowaway)*
Author: Ana María Matute
(Not Translated)

Juju is a child who lives with three unmarried women who adore him. During the day Juju works hard, but at dusk he plays in a small imaginary boat, built in the house's attic, which he calls Ulysses. One morning Juju helps a fugitive from justice who becomes Ulysses's stowaway. They both plan to escape and become free on the seas. This marvelous book holds many insights about dreams and what it means to grow up.
🔍 *Ramón Caraballo, Bookseller*

El príncipe moro. *(The Moorish Prince)*
Author: Fernando Paz Castillo
(Not Translated)

This is the story of a Moorish prince, stripped of his kingdom by an evil fairy. The prince feels a deep sadness and for that reason decides to throw himself into the sea, but at that moment a Moorish fairy appears who helps the prince regain his kingdom, but to do so, he must overcome the evil fairy who lives there and who surely will try to deceive him.
🔍 *Ramón Caraballo, Bookseller*

Sopa de hortalizas = Vegetal Soup.
Author: Ángeles Molina Iturrondo
(Bilingual)

This bilingual story stimulates young readers to the acquisition of language skills. Written by a reading and writing specialist, *Sopa de hortalizas* aids parents and teachers when it comes to involving children in independent reading skills. (English and Spanish).
🔍 *Nashieli Marcano, University of Akron*

La tierra de nadie. *(No Man's Land)*
Author: Alfonso Martínez-Mena
(Not Translated)

In the dark attic exists *No Man's Land*, a mysterious place where children play alongside their grandparents' memories.the room is filled with the dreams of relatives the children could only meet in this imaginative world.
 Teresa Mlawer, Lectorum Publications Inc.

Los tres reyes (a caballo). *(The Three Wise Men (on Horseback))*
Author: Carmen Leonor Rivera Lassen, and Víctor Maldonado Dávila
(Not Translated)

This story is a remake of the ancient tale of the «Three Wise Men»: Melchor, Gaspar and Balthasar. Told in the Puerto Rican folksong style called «décima», the Three Wise Men arrive to the island of Puerto Rico and are welcomed by a horse that helps them disburse their gifts to children all over the island. Ever since this magical trip, the Kings travel through the island on horseback.
 Nashieli Marcano, University of Akron

¡Vamos a jugar! *(Let's Play!)*
Author: Josefina Barceló
(Not Translated)

This collection of games allows children to express their cultural heritage, as well as develop essential social and physical skills. Readers will learn about sportsmanship, how to follow instructions and how to have fun in groups. Included are popular games played in Puerto Rico.
 Nashieli Marcano, University of Akron

Los zapaticos de rosa. *(The Pink Shoes)*
Author: José Martí, and Lulu Delacre, il.
(Not Translated)

While written with delicate simplicity for children to understand, Martí's talent for description makes *Los zapaticos de rosa* so vivid, it is as though the scenes were painted with a brush. This captivating book, masterfully illustrated by Lulu Delacre, is dedicated with tenderness to the young readers for whom José Martí wrote this beautiful poem.
Teresa Mlawer, Lectorum Publications Inc.

El zoo de Pitus. *(Pitus's Zoo)*
Author: Sebastià Sorribas
(Not Translated)

Pitus is a child with many good friends in the neighborhood. When he becomes ill, his family cannot afford the costs of taking him to Sweden, the only place where he might be cured. In order to pay for the trip and the treatment, his friends decide to create a neighborhood zoo for which they will capture all sorts of animals. Translated into several languages, this classic of Catalan children's literature is a beautiful paean to friendship and solidarity.

Lluís Agustí, Instituto Cervantes New York

AUTHORS INDEX

A

Ada, Alma Flor.
Bajo las palmas reales: una infancia cubana — Children / Young Adults
Gathering the Sun: An Alphabet in Spanish and English (Bilingual) — Children / Young Adults
Mi nombre es María Isabel — Children / Young Adults
La moneda de oro — Children / Young Adults

Adoum, Jorge Enrique. Antología poética — Poetry / Drama

Agustín, José.
Cuentos completos (1968-2002) — Literature / Fiction
Tragicomedia mexicana: la vida en México de 1940 a 1970 — Non Fiction

Aira, César. Diccionario de autores latinoamericanos — Reference

Alas «Clarín», Leopoldo. La Regenta — Literature / Fiction

Alatorre, Antonio. Los 1001 años de la lengua española — Non Fiction

Alborg, Juan Luis. Historia de la literatura española — Reference

Aldana, Francisco de. Poesías castellanas completas — Poetry / Drama

Alegría, Fernando. Lautaro, joven libertador de Arauco — Children / Young Adults

Alegría, Ricardo E.
Las primeras representaciones gráficas del indio americano, 1493-1523 — Non Fiction

Alegría Ortega, Idsa E., and Palmira N. Ríos, eds.
Contrapunto de género y raza en Puerto Rico — Non Fiction

Alemán, Mateo. Guzmán de Alfarache — Literature / Fiction

Alfonso X el Sabio. Cantigas de Santa María — Poetry / Drama

Alvar, Carlos, dir. Gran enciclopedia cervantina, v. 1: A buen bocado, buen grito — Reference

Alvar, Carlos, José-Carlos Mainer, and Rosa Navarro.
Breve historia de la literatura española — Non Fiction

Álvarez, Julia. Antes de ser libres — Children / Young Adults

Alvero Francés, Francisco. Lo esencial en la ortografía — Non Fiction

Allende, Isabel.
La casa de los espíritus — Literature / Fiction
La ciudad y las bestias — Children / Young Adults
Eva Luna — Literature / Fiction
Zorro — Literature / Fiction

Anaya, Rudolfo. *Bendíceme, Última* — Literature / Fiction

Anonymus.
Cantar de Mío Cid — Poetry / Drama
El Lazarillo de Tormes — Literature / Fiction
Libro del Caballero Zifar — Literature / Fiction

Aramburu, Fernando. *Los peces de la amargura* — Literature / Fiction

Araujo, Orlando. *Miguel Vicente pata caliente* — Children / Young Adults

Arellano, Jorge Eduardo. *Literatura centroamericana: diccionario de autores centroamericanos: fuentes para su estudio* — Reference

Arenas, Reinaldo.
Antes que anochezca: autobiografía — Literature / Fiction
El mundo alucinante — Literature / Fiction

Arguedas, José María. *Los ríos profundos* — Literature / Fiction

Arias, Martín, and Martín Hadis, eds. *Borges profesor: curso de Literatura inglesa en la Universidad de Buenos Aires* — Non Fiction

Arlt, Roberto. *El juguete rabioso* — Literature / Fiction

Arrabal, Fernando. *Pic-Nic. El triciclo. El laberinto* — Poetry / Drama

Arrom, José Juan. *Mitología y artes prehispánicas de las Antillas* — Non Fiction

Asensi, Matilde. *El último Catón* — Literature / Fiction

Asturias, Miguel Ángel. *El señor Presidente* — Literature / Fiction

Atxaga, Bernardo. *Obabakoak* — Literature / Fiction

Averroes. *Comentario de la Isagogé de Porfirio* — Non Fiction

Ayesta, Julián. *Helena o el mar del verano* — Literature / Fiction

Azuela, Mariano. *Los de abajo* — Literature / Fiction

B

Blanco, José Joaquín, ed. *El lector novohispano*   Literature / Fiction

Bolaño, Roberto.
   2666   Literature / Fiction
   Los detectives salvajes   Literature / Fiction

Bolívar Aróstegui, Natalia. *Los orishas en Cuba*   Non Fiction

Bombal, María Luisa. *La amortajada*   Literature / Fiction

Bonilla, Juan. *El estadio de mármol*   Literature / Fiction

Borau, José Luis, ed. *Diccionario del cine español*   Reference

Borges, Jorge Luis.
   El Aleph   Literature / Fiction
   Ficciones   Literature / Fiction
   Obra poética   Poetry / Drama

Bosch, Juan. *De Cristóbal Colón a Fidel Castro. El Caribe, frontera imperial*   Non Fiction

Bosque, Ignacio, dir. *Redes: diccionario combinatorio del español contemporáneo*   Reference

Bosque, Ignacio, and Violeta Demonte, dirs.
   Gramática descriptiva de la lengua española   Reference

Botaya, Felipe. *Operación Hagen*   Literature / Fiction

Boullosa, Carmen. *La otra mano de Lepanto*   Literature / Fiction

Brown, James W. *Vida moderna hispana*   Non Fiction

Bryce Echenique, Alfredo.
   La amigdalitis de Tarzán   Literature / Fiction
   La vida exagerada de Martín Romaña   Literature / Fiction

C

Caballero Bonald, José Manuel. *Diario de Argónida*   Poetry / Drama

Cabello de Carbonera, Mercedes. *Blanca Sol*   Literature / Fiction

Cabrera Infante, Guillermo. *Tres tristes tigres*   Literature / Fiction

Calderón de la Barca, Pedro. *La vida es sueño*   Poetry / Drama

Cameron, Ann. *Colibrí* — Children / Young Adults

Campoy, F. Isabel, and Alma Flor Ada.
Cuentos que contaban nuestras abuelas — Children / Young Adults

Cané, Miguel. *Juvenilia* — Children / Young Adults

Canetti, Yanitzia.
Ay, luna, luna, lunita... — Children / Young Adults
Completamente diferente — Children / Young Adults

Cardenoso, Concha. *Cuéntame un cuento* — Children / Young Adults

Cardoso, Onelio Jorge. *Negrita* — Children / Young Adults

Cardoza y Aragón, Luis. *El río: novelas de caballería* — Non Fiction

Carpentier, Alejo.
Los pasos perdidos — Literature / Fiction
El recurso del método — Literature / Fiction
El reino de este mundo — Literature / Fiction
El siglo de las luces — Literature / Fiction

Carrera Andrade, Jorge. *Obra poética completa* — Poetry / Drama

Casares, Julio. *Diccionario ideológico de la lengua española* — Reference

Casares Rodicio, Emilio, general coord., José López-Calo, and Ismael Fernández de la Cuesta, dirs.
Diccionario de la música española e hispanoamericana — Reference

Castellanos, Rosario. *Balún Canán* — Literature / Fiction

Castellanos Moya, Horacio. *El Asco: Thomas Bernhard en El Salvador* — Literature / Fiction

Castellet, J.M., selec. *Nueve novísimos poetas españoles* — Poetry / Drama

Castro, Américo. *España en su historia* — Non Fiction

Català, Víctor. *Solitud* — Literature / Fiction

Cela, Camilo José.
La colmena — Literature / Fiction
La familia de Pascual Duarte — Literature / Fiction

Cercas, Javier. *Soldados de Salamina* — Literature / Fiction

Cerón, Rocío, Julián Herbert, and León Plascencia Ñol.
El decir y el vértigo: panorama de la poesía hispanoamericana reciente (1963-1979) — Poetry / Drama

Cervantes, Miguel de.
Don Quijote de la Mancha   Literature / Fiction
Novelas ejemplares   Literature / Fiction
El retablo de las maravillas   Poetry / Drama

Chacel, Rosa. *Barrio de maravillas*   Literature / Fiction

Chang-Rodríguez, Eugenio. *Latinoamérica: su civilización y su cultura*   Non Fiction

Chávez Castañeda, Ricardo.
Crack: instrucciones de uso   Literature / Fiction
Mañanario   Children / Young Adults

Cirlot, Juan Eduardo. *Diccionario de símbolos*   Reference

Cisneros, Sandra. *Caramelo: puro cuento*   Literature / Fiction

Cobián Figeroux, Ricardo. *Anatomía del deseo*   Poetry / Drama

Cobos, Ana María, and Ana Lya Sater.
Latin American Studies: An Annotated Bibliography of Core Works   Reference

Coleman, Alexander. *Cinco maestros: cuentos modernos de Hispanoamérica*   Literature / Fiction

Conde Pen Alosa, Raquel.
Mujeres novelistas y novelas de mujeres en la posguerra española (1940-1965)   Reference

Conget, José María. *Hasta el fin de los cuentos*   Literature / Fiction

Corbeil, Jean-Claude, and Ariane Archambault.
The Firefly Spanish/English Visual Dictionary   Reference

Corominas, Joan. *Diccionario crítico etimológico castellano e hispánico*   Reference

Cortázar, Julio.
Cuentos completos   Literature / Fiction
Historias de cronopios y de famas   Literature / Fiction
Rayuela   Literature / Fiction

Cozarinsky, Edgardo.
La novia de Odessa   Literature / Fiction
El rufián moldavo   Literature / Fiction

Crespo, Ángel. *El bosque transparente (poesía, 1971-1981)*   Poetry / Drama

Cunqueiro, Álvaro. *Las crónicas del sochantre*   Literature / Fiction

D

Da Coll, Ivar.
¡Azúcar!   Children / Young Adults
El día de muertos   Children / Young Adults

Dalton, Roque.
Las historias prohibidas del Pulgarcito   Non Fiction
Poemas clandestinos   Poetry / Drama

Darío, Rubén.
Azul   Poetry / Drama
Azul; España contemporánea; Cantos de vida y esperanza   Poetry / Drama
Cantos de vida y esperanza   Poetry / Drama
Prosas profanas   Poetry / Drama

De Filippis, Daisy Cocco, and Sonia Rivera-Valdéz, eds.
Conversación entre escritoras del Caribe Hispano: Tomo II   Non Fiction

Deive, Carlos Esteban.
La esclavitud del negro en Santo Domingo   Non Fiction
Vudú y magia en Santo Domingo   Non Fiction

Delgado Mercado, Osiris. *Historia general de las artes plásticas en Puerto Rico*   Reference

Delibes, Miguel. *Cinco horas con Mario*   Literature / Fiction

Díaz Alfaro, Abelardo. *Terrazo*   Literature / Fiction

Díaz de Villegas, José. *Puerto Rico la gran cocina del Caribe*   Reference

Donoso, José. *El obsceno pájaro de la noche*   Literature / Fiction

Dubovoy, Silvia. *Cuentos del fondo del mar*   Children / Young Adults

E

Edwards, Jorge. *Persona non grata*   Non Fiction

Egido León, Ángeles. *Manuel Azaña: entre el mito y la leyenda*   Non Fiction

Elizondo, Salvador. *Farabeuf*   Literature / Fiction

F

G

Galarza, Galo. *El turno de Anacle: cuentos*	Literature / Fiction
Galeano, Eduardo. *Las venas abiertas de América Latina*	Non Fiction
Galimberti Jarman, Beatriz, and Roy Russell. *The Oxford Spanish Dictionary: Spanish-English, English-Spanish* = *Gran diccionario Oxford: español-inglés, inglés-español*	Reference
Gallego García, Laura. *Finis mundi*	Children / Young Adults
Gamoneda, Antonio. *El libro del frío*	Poetry / Drama
Gaos, Vicente, ed. *Antología del grupo poético de 1927*	Poetry / Drama
García-Badell, Regino. *Tesoros de la poesía en la lengua castellana*	Poetry / Drama
García Durán, Juan. *La guerra civil española: fuentes (archivos, bibliografía y filmografía)*	Reference
García Lorca, Federico.	
Antología poética	Poetry / Drama
Bodas de sangre	Poetry / Drama
La casa de Bernarda Alba	Poetry / Drama
Poeta en Nueva York	Poetry / Drama
Romancero Gitano	Poetry / Drama
García Márquez, Gabriel.	
El amor en los tiempos de cólera	Literature / Fiction
Cien años de soledad	Literature / Fiction
El coronel no tiene quien le escriba	Literature / Fiction
Vivir para contarla	Non Fiction
García Morales, Adelaida. *El Sur; seguido de Bene*	Literature / Fiction
García Ramis, Magali. *Felices días tío Sergio*	Literature / Fiction
García Riera, Emilio. *Historia documental del cine mexicano*	Reference
García Yebra, Valentín. *Teoría y práctica de la traducción*	Non Fiction
Garcilaso de la Vega. *Poesías castellanas completas*	Poetry / Drama
Garcilaso de la Vega, Inca. *Comentarios Reales*	Non Fiction
Gardea, Jesús. *Reunión de cuentos*	Literature / Fiction
Garmendia, Salvador. *Memorias de Altagracia*	Literature / Fiction

Gibson, Ian. *Federico García Lorca*   Non Fiction

Gil de Biedma, Jaime.
Diario del artista en 1956   Non Fiction
Poemas póstumos   Poetry / Drama
Gironella, José María. *Los cipreses creen en Dios*   Literature / Fiction

Goic, Cedomil, ed. *Historia y crítica de la literatura hispanoamericana*   Reference

Gola, Hugo. *Filtraciones: poemas reunidos*   Poetry / Drama

Góngora, Luis de.
Poesías   Poetry / Drama
Sonetos   Poetry / Drama

González, Ángel. *Palabra sobre palabra: obra completa (1956-2001)*   Poetry / Drama

González, José Luís. *El país de cuatro pisos y otros ensayos*   Non Fiction

González Ledesma, Francisco. *Soldados*   Literature / Fiction

González Rodríguez, Sergio. *Huesos en el desierto*   Non Fiction

Goytisolo, José Agustín. *Antología personal*   Poetry / Drama

Goytisolo, Juan. *Campos de Níjar*   Non Fiction

Gracián, Baltasar. *Oráculo manual y arte de prudencia*   Non Fiction

Granados, Manuel. *Adire y el tiempo roto*   Literature / Fiction

Guillén, Nicolás. *Sóngoro cosongo*   Poetry / Drama

Gullón, Ricardo, dir. *Diccionario de la literatura española e hispanoamericana*   Reference

Gutiérrez, Franklin. *Evas terrenales: biobibliografías de 150 autoras dominicanas*   Reference

Gutiérrez, Pedro Juan. *Trilogía sucia de La Habana*   Literature / Fiction

H

Hayes, Joe. *La Llorona = The Weeping Woman: An Hispanic Legend
Told in Spanish and English (Bilingual)*   Children / Young Adults

Hernández, Felisberto. *Nadie encendía las lámparas y otros cuentos*   Literature / Fiction

Hernández, Miguel. *Cancionero y romancero de ausencias*   Poetry / Drama

Hiriart, Hugo. *Cómo leer y escribir poesía*   Non Fiction

Hirota, Twiggy, ed. *Diccionario de escritores en lengua castellana:*
quién es quién hoy en las letras españolas.   Reference

Huerta Calvo, Javier, Emilio Peral Vega, and Héctor Urzáiz Tortajada.
Teatro español: (de la A a la Z)   Reference

Huidobro, Vicente. *Altazor o el viaje en paracaídas*   Poetry / Drama

Hurtado Albir, Amparo.
Enseñar a traducir: metodología en la formación de traductores e intérpretes   Non Fiction
Traducción y traductología. Introducción a la traductología   Non Fiction

I

Ibarbourou, Juana de. *Las lenguas de diamante / Raíz salvaje*   Poetry / Drama

Imbert Brugal, Carmen. *Distinguida Señora*   Literature / Fiction

Instituto Cervantes.
El español en el mundo: anuario del Instituto Cervantes   Reference
Plan curricular del Instituto Cervantes: niveles de referencia para el español   Reference

Isol. *Cosas que pasan*   Children / Young Adults

J

Jarque, Fietta. *Yo me perdono*   Literature / Fiction

Jarvis, Ana C., Raquel Lebredo, and Francisco Mena-Ayllón.
Aventuras literarias   Literature / Fiction

Jiménez, Juan Ramón.
Animal de fondo   Poetry / Drama
Platero y yo   Literature / Fiction

Juan de la Cruz, San. *Obras escogidas*   Poetry / Drama

Juan Manuel, Infante de Castilla. *El libro del Conde Lucanor*   Literature / Fiction

Juana Inés de la Cruz, Sor. *Respuesta a Sor Filotea*   Non Fiction

K

Kahlo, Frida. *Escrituras de Frida Kahlo* — Non Fiction

Kanellos, Nicolas, ed. *Herencia: The Anthology of Hispanic Literature of the United States (Bilingual)* — Literature / Fiction

Kattan Ibarra, Juan.
Panorama de la prensa: temas contemporáneos del mundo hispano — Non Fiction
Perspectivas culturales de Hispanoamérica — Non Fiction

Kuri-Aldana, Mario, and Vicente Mendoza Martínez.
Cancionero popular mexicano — Non Fiction

L

Laforet, Carmen. *Nada* — Literature / Fiction

Lago, Eduardo. *Llámame Brooklyn* — Literature / Fiction

Laguerre, Enrique. *Residuos de los tiempos* — Poetry / Drama

Lantigua, José Rafael. *Semblanzas del corazón* — Literature / Fiction

Larra, Mariano José de. *Artículos* — Non Fiction

Larrea, Juan. *Versión celeste* — Poetry / Drama

Lastra, Pedro. *Noticias del extranjero* — Poetry / Drama

Lázaro, Georgina.
El flamboyán amarillo — Children / Young Adults
Julia — Children / Young Adults

Lázaro Carreter, Fernando. *El dardo en la palabra* — Non Fiction

Lemebel, Pedro. *Tengo miedo torero* — Literature / Fiction

León, María Teresa. *Memoria de la melancolía* — Non Fiction

Lezama Lima, José. *Paradiso* — Literature / Fiction

Lindo, Elvira. *Una palabra tuya* — Literature / Fiction

López de Mendoza, Íñigo, Marqués de Santillana. *Obra poética* — Poetry / Drama

López Guix, Gabriel, and J. Minnet Wilkinson.
Manual de traducción inglés/castellano — Non Fiction

López y Fuentes, Gregorio. *El Indio* — Literature / Fiction

Luis de León, Fray. *Poesía* — Poetry / Drama

Llamazares, Julio. *La lluvia amarilla* — Literature / Fiction

M

Machado, Antonio.
Antología poética — Poetry / Drama
Campos de Castilla — Poetry / Drama

Manrique, Jorge. *Poesía* — Poetry / Drama

Mansour Manzur, Vivian.
El enmascarado de lata — Children / Young Adults
El peinado de la tía Chofi — Children / Young Adults

March, Ausiàs. *Poesía* — Poetry / Drama

Marechal, Leopoldo. *Adán Buenosayres* — Literature / Fiction

Margarit, Joan. *Antología poética* — Poetry / Drama

Marsé, Juan. *Si te dicen que caí* — Literature / Fiction

Martí, José. *Los zapaticos de rosa* — Children / Young Adults

Martín Gaite, Carmen.
El cuarto de atrás — Literature / Fiction
Entre visillos — Literature / Fiction
Nubosidad variable — Literature / Fiction

Martín Vivaldi, Gonzalo.
Curso de redacción. Teoría y práctica de la composición y del estilo — Non Fiction

Martínez, Guillermo. *La mujer del maestro* — Literature / Fiction

Martínez, Rubén. *Cruzando la frontera: la crónica implacable de una familia mexicana que emigra a Estados Unidos* — Non Fiction

Martínez, Tomás Eloy. *El vuelo de la reina* — Literature / Fiction

Martínez-Mena, Alfonso. *La tierra de nadie* — Children / Young Adults

Martínez de Sousa, José. *Diccionario de bibliología y ciencias afines: terminología relativa a archivística, artes e industrias gráficas, bibliofilia, bibliografía, bibliología, bibliotecología.* — Reference
Ortografía y ortotipografía del español actual — Reference

Martorell, Joanot. *Tirant lo Blanc* — Literature / Fiction

Mastretta, Ángeles.
Arráncame la vida — Literature / Fiction
Mujeres de ojos grandes — Literature / Fiction

Mateo Díez, Luis. *El oscurecer* — Literature / Fiction

Mateos, Pilar. *Historias de ninguno* — Children / Young Adults

Matute, Ana María. *El polizón del Ulises* — Children / Young Adults

Mejía, José, ed. *Los centroamericanos: antología de cuentos* — Literature / Fiction

Méndez, Alberto. *Los girasoles ciegos* — Literature / Fiction

Mendoza Díaz-Maroto, Francisco.
La pasión por los libros: un acercamiento a la bibliofilia — Non Fiction

Mendoza, Eduardo.
La ciudad de los prodigios — Literature / Fiction
El misterio de la cripta embrujada — Literature / Fiction
Sin noticias de Gurb — Literature / Fiction

Miró, Ricardo. *Poesía selecta* — Poetry / Drama

Mistral, Gabriela. *Tala* — Poetry / Drama

Molina, César Antonio. *El rumor del tiempo* — Poetry / Drama

Molina, Silvia. *Le comieron la lengua los ratones* — Children / Young Adults

Molina, Tirso de. *El burlador de Sevilla* — Poetry / Drama

Molina Iturrondo, Ángeles. *Sopa de hortalizas = Vegetal Soup* — Children / Young Adults

Moliner, María. *Diccionario del uso del español* — Reference

Monsiváis, Carlos, ed. *Lo fugitivo permanece. 20 cuentos mexicanos.* — Literature / Fiction

Montejo, Eugenio. *El azul de la tierra* — Poetry / Drama

Montero, Rosa. *El corazón del tártaro*	Literature / Fiction
Monterroso, Augusto. *Obras completas (y otros cuentos)*	Literature / Fiction
Montes, Marisa. *Juan Bobo busca trabajo*	Children / Young Adults
Mora, Pat. *Una biblioteca para Juana: el mundo de Sor Juana Inés*	Children / Young Adults
Moral, Rafael del. *Enciclopedia de la novela española*	Reference
Morant, Isabel, dir. *Historia de las mujeres en España y América Latina*	Reference
Moreno Cabrera, Juan Carlos. *El universo de las lenguas: clasificación, denominación, situación, tipología, historia y bibliografía de las lenguas*	Reference

Mújica Láinez, Manuel.
Bomarzo — Literature / Fiction
Misteriosa Buenos Aires — Literature / Fiction

Mullen, Edward J., and John E. Garganigo.
El cuento hispánico: A Graded Literary Anthology — Literature / Fiction

Muñoz-Alonso López, Agustín, ed. *Teatro español de vanguardia* — Poetry / Drama

Muñoz Martín, Juan. *Fray Perico y su borrico* — Children / Young Adults

Muñoz Molina, Antonio.
Córdoba de los omeyas — Non Fiction
El invierno en Lisboa — Literature / Fiction
El jinete polaco — Literature / Fiction
El viento de la luna — Literature / Fiction

Mutis, Álvaro. *La última escala del Tramp Steamer* — Literature / Fiction

N

Nava, Michael. *El chico de oro* — Literature / Fiction

Navarro, Justo. *Hermana muerte* — Literature / Fiction

Nazario, Sonia. *La travesía de Enrique* — Non Fiction

Neruda, Pablo.
Cien sonetos de amor — Poetry / Drama
Confieso que he vivido — Non Fiction
Veinte poemas de amor y una canción desesperada — Poetry / Drama

Neuman, Andrés, ed.
Pequeñas resistencias: antología del nuevo cuento español   Literature / Fiction

Nogueras, Paola. *ABC de Puerto Rico*   Children / Young Adults

Nolla, Olga. *Rosas de papel*   Literature / Fiction

Novás Calvo, Lino. *Cayo Canas*   Literature / Fiction

Núñez Cabeza de Vaca, Alvar. *Naufragios y Comentarios*   Non Fiction

O

Ocampo, Silvina. *Cuentos completos*   Literature / Fiction

Oliver Labra, Carilda. *Al sur de mi garganta*   Poetry / Drama

Ollero, Julio, and Susana Bardón, eds.
El mercado del libro antiguo español: una guía de precios   Reference

Oquendo de Amat, Carlos. *5 metros de poemas*   Poetry / Drama

Ors, Eugeni d´. *La Bien Plantada*   Non Fiction

Ortega y Gasset, José.
Misión del bibliotecario y otros ensayos afines   Non Fiction
La rebelión de las masas   Non Fiction

Ortiz, Fernando. *Los instrumentos de la música afrocubana*   Reference

Otero Silva, Miguel. *Oficina N° 1*   Literature / Fiction

P

Pacheco, José Emilio. *Las batallas del desierto*   Literature / Fiction

Padura, Leonardo. *Adiós Hemingway*   Literature / Fiction

Palau y Dulcet, Antonio. *Manual del librero hispanoamericano*   Reference

Palés Matos, Luis. *Tuntún de pasa y grifería*   Poetry / Drama

Pané, Ramón, Fray, and José Juan Arrom, ed.
Relación acerca de las antigüedades de los indios   Non Fiction

Paranaguá, Paulo Antonio. *Cine documental en América Latina*	Reference
Paszkowski, Diego. *Tesis de un homicidio*	Literature / Fiction
Paz Castillo, Fernando. *El príncipe moro*	Children / Young Adults
Paz, Octavio.	
El laberinto de la soledad	Non Fiction
Traducción: literatura y literalidad	Non Fiction
Paz Soldán, Edmundo. *El delirio de Turing*	Literature / Fiction
Perera, Hilda.	
Cuentos para chicos y grandes	Children / Young Adults
Pedrín y la garza	Children / Young Adults
Perdido	Children / Young Adults
Pereyra, Emilia. *Cenizas del querer*	Literature / Fiction
Pérez Díaz, Enrique. *El niño que conversaba con la mar*	Children / Young Adults
Pérez Galdós, Benito. *Fortunata y Jacinta: dos historias de casadas*	Literature / Fiction
Pérez Perucha, Julio, ed. *Antología crítica del cine español: 1906-1995*	Reference
Pérez-Reverte, Arturo.	
El Club Dumas	Literature / Fiction
La reina del sur	Literature / Fiction
Peri Rossi, Cristina. *La última noche de Dostoievski*	Literature / Fiction
Pfeiffer, Rubin.	
Cuentitos simpáticos: A Graded Reader for Advanced Beginning Students	Literature / Fiction
Picó, Fernando. *La peineta colorada*	Children / Young Adults
Piglia, Ricardo.	
Crítica y ficción	Non Fiction
Respiración artificial	Literature / Fiction
Pinilla, Ramiro. *La higuera*	Literature / Fiction
Piñera, Virgilio. *La carne de René*	Literature / Fiction
Pizarnik, Alejandra. *Obras completas: poesía completa y prosa selecta*	Poetry / Drama
Pla, Josefina. *Antología poética*	Poetry / Drama

Q

R

Reviejo, Carlos. *Platero y Juan Ramón*   Children / Young Adults

Reyes, Alfonso. *Visión de Anáhuac y otros ensayos*   Non Fiction

Reyes, Edwin. *El arpa imaginaria*   Poetry / Drama

Reynal, Vicente.
Diccionario de hombres y mujeres ilustres de Puerto Rico y de hechos históricos   Reference

Ribeyro, Julio Ramón. *Antología personal*   Literature / Fiction

Rico, Francisco, ed. *Historia y crítica de la literatura española*   Reference

Ridruejo, Dionisio. *Cuadernos de Rusia*   Non Fiction

Riera, Carme. *En el último azul*   Literature / Fiction

Ríos Ávila, Rubén. *La raza cómica: del sujeto en Puerto Rico*   Non Fiction

Rivas, Manuel.
El lápiz del carpintero   Literature / Fiction
Los libros arden mal   Literature / Fiction

Rivera, José Eustaquio. *La vorágine*   Literature / Fiction

Rivera de Álvarez, Josefina. *Literatura puertorriqueña: su proceso en el tiempo*   Reference

Rivera Lassen, Carmen Leonor, and Víctor Maldonado Dávila.
Los tres reyes (a caballo)   Children / Young Adults

Rivers, Elias L. *Renaissance and Baroque Poetry of Spain (Bilingual)*   Poetry / Drama

Roa Bastos, Augusto. *Yo el supremo*   Literature / Fiction

Rodgers, Eamonn, ed. *Encyclopedia of Contemporary Spanish Culture*   Reference

Rodoreda, Mercè. *La plaza del diamante*   Literature / Fiction

Rodríguez Almodóvar, Antonio. *Cuentos al amor de la lumbre*   Children / Young Adults

Rojas, Fernando de. *La Celestina*   Poetry / Drama

Rojas, Manuel. *Hijo de ladrón*   Literature / Fiction

Ruiz, Juan, Arcipreste de Hita. *Libro de buen amor*   Poetry / Drama

Ruiz de Alarcón, Juan. *La verdad sospechosa* — Literature / Fiction

Ruiz Zafón, Carlos.
El palacio de la medianoche — Children / Young Adults
La sombra del viento — Literature / Fiction

Rulfo, Juan. *Pedro Páramo* — Literature / Fiction

S

Saer, Juan José. *El entenado* — Literature / Fiction

Sagarra, Josep Maria de. *Memorias* — Non Fiction

Sales, Joan. *Incierta gloria* — Literature / Fiction

Salinas, Jaime. *Travesías* — Non Fiction

Sampedro, José Luis. *La sonrisa etrusca* — Literature / Fiction

Sánchez, Carlos Cuauhtémoc. *Juventud en éxtasis* — Literature / Fiction

Sánchez, Luis Rafael. *La guaracha del Macho Camacho* — Literature / Fiction

Sánchez Ferlosio, Rafael. *Industrias y andanzas de Alfanhuí* — Literature / Fiction

Sánchez Piñol, Albert. *La piel fría* — Literature / Fiction

Scarano, Francisco. *Puerto Rico, cinco siglos de historia* — Reference

Seco, Manuel.
Diccionario de dudas y dificultades de la lengua española — Reference
Diccionario fraseológico documentado del español actual: locuciones y modismos — Reference

Semprún, Jorge.
Autobiografía de Federico Sánchez — Non Fiction
El largo viaje — Non Fiction

Sención, Viriato. *Los que falsificaron la firma de Dios* — Literature / Fiction

Sender, Ramón J.
Imán — Literature / Fiction
Réquiem por un campesino español — Literature / Fiction

Sepúlveda, Luis. *Historia de una gaviota y del gato que le enseñó a volar* — Literature / Fiction

Serna, Enrique. *Amores de segunda mano* — Literature / Fiction

Serra Deliz, Wenceslao.
En las cavernas de Camuy: Terón y su maravilloso mundo subterráneo — Children / Young Adults

Serrano, Marcela. *Lo que está en mi corazón* — Literature / Fiction

Sinán, Rogelio. *Plenilunio* — Literature / Fiction

Skármeta, Antonio. *El cartero de Neruda: ardiente paciencia* — Literature / Fiction

Skirius, John, ed. *El ensayo hispanoamericano del siglo XX* — Non Fiction

Soler, Jordi. *Los rojos de ultramar* — Literature / Fiction

Sorribas, Sebastià. *El zoo de Pitus* — Children / Young Adults

Soto, Pedro Juan. *Spiks* — Literature / Fiction

Stavans, Ilan, ed., and Harold Augenbraum, assoc. ed.
Encyclopedia Latina: History, Culture and Society in the United States — Reference

Suances-Torres, Jaime. *Diccionario del verbo español, hispanoamericano y dialectal* — Reference

T

Taboada Terán, Néstor. *Indios en rebelión* — Literature / Fiction

Tenembaum, Barbara A., and Georgette M. Dorn, eds.
Encyclopedia of Latin American History and Culture — Reference

Teresa de Jesús, Santa. *El castillo interior o las moradas* — Poetry / Drama

Toro-Sugrañés, José A. *Nueva enciclopedia de Puerto Rico* — Reference

U

Umbral, Francisco. *Larra, anatomía de un dandy* — Non Fiction

Unamuno, Miguel de.
Del sentimiento trágico de la vida — Non Fiction
Niebla — Literature / Fiction
San Manuel Bueno Mártir — Literature / Fiction

Uribe, María de la Luz. *Doña Piñones* — Children / Young Adults

V

Valdelomar, Abraham. *Los ojos de Judas y otros cuentos*	Literature / Fiction
Valdés, Zoé. *Café nostalgia*	Literature / Fiction
Valente, José Ángel.	
Anatomía de la palabra	Poetry / Drama
No amanece el cantor	Poetry / Drama
Valle, Rafael Heliodoro. *La rosa intemporal*	Poetry / Drama
Valle-Inclán, Ramón María del. *Luces de bohemia*	Poetry / Drama
Vallejo, César. *Trilce*	Poetry / Drama
Valverde, Mikel. *Paula en Nueva York*	Children / Young Adults
Vargas Llosa, Mario.	
La ciudad y los perros	Literature / Fiction
Conversación en la catedral	Literature / Fiction
Los cuadernos de don Rigoberto	Literature / Fiction
La fiesta del Chivo	Literature / Fiction
El hablador	Literature / Fiction
La orgía perpetua	Non Fiction
Pantaleón y las visitadoras	Literature / Fiction
El pez en en el agua: memorias	Non Fiction
Travesuras de la niña mala	Literature / Fiction
Vázquez-Ayora, Gerardo. *Introducción a la traductología*	Non Fiction
Vázquez, Ángel. *La vida perra de Juanita Narboni*	Literature / Fiction
Vázquez, Lourdes. *Sin ti no soy yo*	Literature / Fiction
Vázquez Montalbán, Manuel. *Galíndez*	Literature / Fiction
Vega, Ana Lydia. *Vírgenes y mártires*	Literature / Fiction
Vega, Lope de.	
Fuenteovejuna	Poetry / Drama
Poesías líricas	Poetry / Drama
Velásquez Guzmán, Mónica, ed.	
Antología de la poesía boliviana: ordenar la danza	Poetry / Drama

Veloz Maggiolo, Marcio. *Materia Prima: protonovela*	Literature / Fiction
Vergés, Pedro. *Sólo cenizas hallarás (bolero)*	Literature / Fiction
Vicent, Manuel. *Son de mar*	Literature / Fiction
Vidal, César. *Diccionario del Quijote: la obra para entender uno de los libros esenciales de la cultura universal*	Reference
Vila-Matas, Enrique. *Hijos sin hijos*	Literature / Fiction
Vila-Sanjuán, Sergio. *Pasando página: autores y editores en la España democrática*	Non Fiction
Villena, Luis Antonio de. *El mal mundo*	Literature / Fiction
Villoro, Juan. *Las golosinas secretas*	Children / Young Adults
El testigo	Literature / Fiction
Volpi, Jorge. *No será la tierra*	Literature / Fiction

WYZ

Walsh, María Elena. *Pocopán*	Children / Young Adults
Yañez Cossío, Alicia. *El Cristo feo*	Literature / Fiction
Zeno Gandía, Manuel. *La charca*	Literature / Fiction

TITLES INDEX

# #

5 metros de poemas / Carlos Oquendo de Amat.	Poetry / Drama
Los 1001 años de la lengua española / Antonio Alatorre.	Non Fiction
2666 / Roberto Bolaño.	Literature / Fiction
50.000 nombres para su bebé / Equipo Editorial.	Reference

A

A la deriva y otros cuentos / Horacio Quiroga.	Literature / Fiction
ABC de Puerto Rico / Paola Nogueras.	Children / Young Adults
Adán Buenosayres / Leopoldo Marechal.	Literature / Fiction
Adiós Hemingway / Leonardo Padura.	Literature / Fiction
Adire y el tiempo roto / Manuel Granados.	Literature / Fiction
Al sur de mi garganta / Carilda Oliver Labra.	Poetry / Drama
El Aleph / Jorge Luis Borges.	Literature / Fiction
Altazor o el viaje en paracaídas / Vicente Huidobro.	Poetry / Drama
La amigdalitis de Tarzán / Alfredo Bryce Echenique.	Literature / Fiction
El amor en los tiempos de cólera / Gabriel García Márquez.	Literature / Fiction
Amores de segunda mano / Enrique Serna.	Literature / Fiction
La amortajada / María Luisa Bombal.	Literature / Fiction
Anatomía de la palabra / José Ángel Valente.	Poetry / Drama
Anatomía del deseo / Ricardo Cobián Figeroux.	Poetry / Drama
Animal de fondo / Juan Ramón Jiménez.	Poetry / Drama
Antes de ser libres / Julia Álvarez.	Children / Young Adults
Antes que anochezca: autobiografía / Reinaldo Arenas.	Literature / Fiction

Antología crítica del cine español: 1906-1995 / Julio Pérez Perucha, ed.	Reference
Antología de la poesía boliviana: ordenar la danza / Mónica Velásquez Guzmán, ed.	Poetry / Drama
Antología del grupo poético de 1927 / Vicente Gaos, ed.	Poetry / Drama
Antología personal / José Agustín Goytisolo.	Poetry / Drama
Antología personal / Julio Ramón Ribeyro.	Literature / Fiction
Antología poética / Antonio Machado.	Poetry / Drama
Antología poética / Federico García Lorca.	Poetry / Drama
Antología poética / Jorge Enrique Adoum.	Poetry / Drama
Antología poética / Josefina Pla.	Poetry / Drama
Antología poética / Joan Margarit.	Poetry / Drama
El árbol de la ciencia / Pío Baroja.	Literature / Fiction
El arpa imaginaria / Edwin Reyes.	Poetry / Drama
Arráncame la vida / Ángeles Mastretta.	Literature / Fiction
Artículos / Mariano José de Larra.	Non Fiction
El Asco: Thomas Bernhard en El Salvador / Horacio Castellanos Moya.	Literature / Fiction
Autobiografía de Federico Sánchez / Jorge Semprún.	Non Fiction
Aventuras literarias / Ana C. Jarvis, Raquel Lebredo, and Francisco Mena-Ayllón.	Literature / Fiction
Ay, luna, luna, lunita... / Yanitzia Canetti, and Ángeles Peinador, il.	Children / Young Adults
¡Azúcar! / Ivar Da Coll.	Children / Young Adults
Azul / Rubén Darío.	Poetry / Drama
El azul de la tierra / Eugenio Montejo.	Poetry / Drama
Azul; España contemporánea; Cantos de vida y esperanza / Rubén Darío.	Poetry / Drama

B

Bajo las palmas reales: una infancia cubana / Alma Flor Ada.	Children / Young Adults
Balún Canán / Rosario Castellanos.	Literature / Fiction
Barrio de maravillas / Rosa Chacel.	Literature / Fiction
Las batallas del desierto / José Emilio Pacheco.	Literature / Fiction
Bendíceme, Última / Rudolfo Anaya.	Literature / Fiction
El beso de la mujer araña / Manuel Puig.	Literature / Fiction
Una biblioteca para Juana: el mundo de Sor Juana Inés / Pat Mora.	Children / Young Adults
La Bien Plantada / Eugeni d´Ors.	Non Fiction
Biografía de un cimarrón / Miguel Barnet.	Non Fiction
Blanca Sol / Mercedes Cabello de Carbonera.	Literature / Fiction
Bodas de sangre / Federico García Lorca.	Poetry / Drama
Bomarzo / Manuel Mújica Láinez.	Literature / Fiction
Borges profesor: curso de Literatura inglesa en la Universidad de Buenos Aires / Martín Arias, and Martín Hadis, eds.	Non Fiction
El bosque transparente (poesía, 1971-1981) / Crespo, Ángel.	Poetry / Drama
Breve historia de la literatura española / Carlos Alvar, José-Carlos Mainer, and Rosa Navarro.	Non Fiction
El burlador de Sevilla / Tirso de Molina.	Poetry / Drama
Buscando un Inca: identidad y utopía en los Andes / Alberto Flores Galindo.	Non Fiction

C

Caballo de Troya / J.J. Benítez.	Literature / Fiction
Café nostalgia / Zoé Valdés.	Literature / Fiction
La caja negra / Juan Carlos Quintero.	Poetry / Drama
Campos de Castilla / Antonio Machado.	Poetry / Drama

Campos de Níjar / Juan Goytisolo.	Non Fiction
Cancionero popular mexicano / Mario Kuri-Aldana, and Vicente Mendoza Martínez.	Non Fiction
Cancionero y romancero de ausencias / Miguel Hernández.	Poetry / Drama
Cantar de Mío Cid / Anonymous.	Poetry / Drama
Cantigas de Santa María / Alfonso X el Sabio.	Poetry / Drama
Cantos de vida y esperanza / Rubén Darío.	Poetry / Drama
Caramelo: puro cuento / Sandra Cisneros.	Literature / Fiction
La carne de René / Virgilio Piñera.	Literature / Fiction
El cartero de Neruda: ardiente paciencia / Antonio Skármeta.	Literature / Fiction
La casa de Bernarda Alba / Federico García Lorca.	Poetry / Drama
La casa de la laguna / Rosario Ferré.	Literature / Fiction
La casa de los espíritus / Isabel Allende.	Literature / Fiction
El castillo interior o las moradas / Santa Teresa de Jesús.	Poetry / Drama
La catedral del mar / Ildefonso Falcones.	Literature / Fiction
Cayo Canas / Lino Novás Calvo.	Literature / Fiction
La cazadora de Indiana Jones / Asun Balzola.	Children / Young Adults
La Celestina / Fernando de Rojas.	Poetry / Drama
Cenizas del querer / Emilia Pereyra.	Literature / Fiction
Los centroamericanos: antología de cuentos / José Mejía, ed.	Literature / Fiction
La charca / Manuel Zeno Gandía.	Literature / Fiction
El chico de oro / Michael Nava.	Literature / Fiction
Cien años de soledad / Gabriel García Márquez.	Literature / Fiction
Cien sonetos de amor / Pablo Neruda.	Poetry / Drama

Cinco horas con Mario / Miguel Delibes.	Literature / Fiction
Cinco maestros: cuentos modernos de Hispanoamérica / Alexander Coleman.	Literature / Fiction
Cine argentino / Claudio España, ed.	Reference
Cine documental en América Latina / Paulo Antonio Paranaguá.	Reference
Los cipreses creen en Dios / José María Gironella.	Literature / Fiction
La ciudad de los prodigios / Eduardo Mendoza.	Literature / Fiction
La ciudad y las bestias / Isabel Allende.	Children / Young Adults
La ciudad y los perros / Mario Vargas Llosa.	Literature / Fiction
El Club Dumas / Arturo Pérez-Reverte.	Literature / Fiction
Colibrí / Ann Cameron.	Children / Young Adults
La colmena / Camilo José Cela.	Literature / Fiction
Comentario de la Isagogé de Porfirio / Averroes.	Non Fiction
Comentarios Reales / Inca Garcilaso de la Vega.	Non Fiction
Como agua para chocolate / Laura Esquivel.	Literature / Fiction
Cómo leer y escribir poesía / Hugo Hiriart.	Non Fiction
Completamente diferente / Yanitzia Canetti, and Ángeles Peinador, il.	Children / Young Adults
Condenados de Condado / Norberto Fuentes.	Literature / Fiction
Confieso que he vivido / Pablo Neruda.	Non Fiction
Conspiración Maine / Mario Escobar Golderos.	Literature / Fiction
Contrapunto de género y raza en Puerto Rico / Idsa E. Alegría Ortega, and Palmira N. Ríos, eds.	Non Fiction
Conversación en la catedral / Mario Vargas Llosa.	Literature / Fiction
Conversación entre escritoras del Caribe Hispano: Tomo II / Daisy Cocco De Filippis, and Sonia Rivera-Valdéz, eds.	Non Fiction

Cuentos para chicos y grandes / Hilda Perera, and Rapi Diego, il.	Children / Young Adults
Cuentos que contaban nuestras abuelas / F. Isabel Campoy, and Alma Flor Ada.	Children / Young Adults
Curso de redacción. Teoría y práctica de la composición y del estilo / Gonzalo Martín Vivaldi.	Non Fiction

D

El dardo en la palabra / Fernando Lázaro Carreter.	Non Fiction
Los de abajo / Mariano Azuela.	Literature / Fiction
De Cristóbal Colón a Fidel Castro. El Caribe, frontera imperial / Juan Bosch.	Non Fiction
El decir y el vértigo: panorama de la poesía hispanoamericana reciente (1963-1979) / Rocío Cerón, Julián Herbert, and León Plascencia Ñol.	Poetry / Drama
Del sentimiento trágico de la vida / Miguel de Unamuno.	Non Fiction
Delirio / Laura Restrepo.	Literature / Fiction
El delirio de Turing / Edmundo Paz Soldán.	Literature / Fiction
Los detectives salvajes / Roberto Bolaño.	Literature / Fiction
El día de muertos / Ivar Da Coll.	Children / Young Adults
Diario de Argónida / José Manuel Caballero Bonald.	Poetry / Drama
Diario del artista en 1956 / Jaime Gil de Biedma.	Non Fiction
Diccionario crítico etimológico castellano e hispánico / Joan Corominas.	Reference
Diccionario de autores latinoamericanos / César Aira.	Reference
Diccionario de bibliología y ciencias afines: terminología relativa a archivística, artes e industrias gráficas, bibliofilia, bibliografía, bibliología, bibliotecología. / José Martínez de Sousa.	Reference
Diccionario de dudas y dificultades de la lengua española / Manuel Seco.	Reference
Diccionario de escritores en lengua castellana: quién es quién hoy en las letras españolas. / Twiggy Hirota, ed.	Reference

Diccionario de hombres y mujeres ilustres de Puerto Rico y de hechos históricos / Vicente Reynal.   Reference

Diccionario de la lengua española / Real Academia Española.   Reference

Diccionario de la literatura española e hispanoamericana / Ricardo Gullón, dir.   Referenc

Diccionario de la música española e hispanoamericana / Emilio Casares Rodicio, dir. and general coord., José López-Calo and Ismael Fernández de la Cuesta, dirs.   Reference

Diccionario de símbolos / Juan Eduardo Cirlot.   Reference

Diccionario del cine español / José Luis Borau, ed.   Reference

Diccionario del Quijote: la obra para entender uno de los libros esenciales de la cultura universal / César Vidal.   Reference

Diccionario del uso del español / María Moliner.   Reference

Diccionario del verbo español, hispanoamericano y dialectal / Jaime Suances-Torres.   Reference

Diccionario fraseológico documentado del español actual: locuciones y modismos / Manuel Seco.   Reference

Diccionario ideológico de la lengua española / Julio Casares.   Reference

Diccionario panhispánico de dudas / Real Academia Española.   Reference

Distinguida Señora / Carmen Imbert Brugal.   Literature / Fiction

Don Quijote de la Mancha / Miguel de Cervantes.   Literature / Fiction

Doña Piñones / María de la Luz Uribe.   Children / Young Adults

E

En busca del unicornio / Juan Eslava Galán.   Literature / Fiction

En el último azul / Carme Riera.   Literature / Fiction

En las cavernas de Camuy: Terón y su maravilloso mundo subterráneo / Wenceslao Serra Deliz.   Children / Young Adults

Enciclopedia de la novela española / Rafael del Moral.   Reference

Enciclopedia Hispánica / Encyclopaedia Britannica.   Reference

Encyclopedia Latina: History, Culture and Society in the United States /
Ilan Stavans, editor in chief, and Harold Augenbraum, associate editor.   Reference

Encyclopedia of Contemporary Latin American and Caribbean Cultures /
Daniel Balderston, Mike Gonzalez, and Ana M. López, eds.   Reference

Encyclopedia of Contemporary Spanish Culture / Eamonn Rodgers, ed.   Reference

Encyclopedia of Latin American History and Culture /
Barbara A. Tenembaum, and Georgette M. Dorn, eds.   Reference

El enmascarado de lata / Vivian Mansour Manzur, and Trino, il.   Children / Young Adults

El ensayo hispanoamericano del siglo XX / John Skirius, ed.   Non Fiction

*Enseñar a traducir: metodología en la formación de
traductores e intérpretes* / Amparo Hurtado Albir.   Non Fiction

El entenado / Juan José Saer.   Literature / Fiction

Entre visillos / Carmen Martín Gaite.   Literature / Fiction

La esclavitud del negro en Santo Domingo / Carlos Esteban Deive.   Non Fiction

Escrituras de Frida Kahlo / Frida Kahlo.   Non Fiction

Escuela de mandarines / Miguel Espinosa.   Literature / Fiction

España en su historia / Américo Castro.   Non Fiction

El español en el mundo: anuario del Instituto Cervantes / Instituto Cervantes.   Reference

El estadio de mármol / Juan Bonilla.   Literature / Fiction

Eva Luna / Isabel Allende.   Literature / Fiction

Evas terrenales: biobibliografías de 150 autoras dominicanas /
Franklin Gutiérrez.   Reference

F

La familia de Pascual Duarte / Camilo José Cela.   Literature / Fiction

Farabeuf / Salvador Elizondo.   Literature / Fiction

Federico García Lorca / Ian Gibson.   Non Fiction

Felices días tío Sergio / Magali García Ramis.	Literature / Fiction
La fiesta del Chivo / Mario Vargas Llosa.	Literature / Fiction
Filtraciones: poemas reunidos / Hugo Gola.	Poetry / Drama
Finis mundi / Laura Gallego García.	Children / Young Adults
The Firefly Spanish/English Visual Dictionary / Jean-Claude Corbeil, and Ariane Archambault.	Reference
El flamboyán amarillo / Georgina Lázaro, and Lulu Delacre, il.	Children / Young Adults
La forja de un rebelde / Arturo Barea.	Literature / Fiction
Fortunata y Jacinta: dos historias de casadas / Benito Pérez Galdós.	Literature / Fiction
Franco, Caudillo de España / Paul Preston.	Non Fiction
Fray Perico y su borrico / Juan Muñoz Martín.	Children / Young Adults
Fuenteovejuna / Lope de Vega.	Poetry / Drama

G

Galíndez / Manuel Vázquez Montalbán.	Literature / Fiction
Gathering the Sun: An Alphabet in Spanish and English / Alma Flor Ada.	Children / Young Adults
Los girasoles ciegos / Alberto Méndez.	Literature / Fiction
Las golosinas secretas / Juan Villoro, and Mauricio Gómez Morin, il.	Children / Young Adults
Gramática de la lengua castellana dedicada al uso de los americanos / Andrés Bello.	Reference
Gramática descriptiva de la lengua española / Ignacio Bosque, and Violeta Demonte, dirs.	Reference
Gran diccionario Oxford: español-inglés, inglés-español = The Oxford Spanish Dictionary: Spanish-English, English-Spanish / Beatriz Galimberti Jarman, and Roy Russell.	Reference
Gran enciclopedia cervantina, v. 1: A buen bocado, buen grito / Carlos Alvar, dir.	Reference

H

Historia documental del cine mexicano / Emilio García Riera.	Reference
Historia general de las artes plásticas en Puerto Rico / Osiris Delgado Mercado.	Reference
Historia y crítica de la literatura española / Francisco Rico, ed.	Reference
Historia y crítica de la literatura hispanoamericana / Cedomil Goic, ed.	Reference
Historias de cronopios y de famas / Julio Cortázar.	Literature / Fiction
Historias de ninguno / Pilar Mateos.	Children / Young Adults
Las historias prohibidas del Pulgarcito / Roque Dalton.	Non Fiction
Huesos en el desierto / Sergio González Rodríguez.	Non Fiction

I

Imán / Ramón J. Sender.	Literature / Fiction
Incierta gloria / Joan Sales.	Literature / Fiction
El Indio / Gregorio López y Fuentes.	Literature / Fiction
Indios en rebelión / Néstor Taboada Terán.	Literature / Fiction
Industrias y andanzas de Alfanhuí / Rafael Sánchez Ferlosio.	Literature / Fiction
Las inquietudes de Shanti Andía / Pío Baroja.	Literature / Fiction
Los instrumentos de la música afrocubana / Fernando Ortiz.	Reference
Introducción a la traductología / Gerardo Vázquez-Ayora.	Non Fiction
La invención de Morel / Adolfo Bioy Casares.	Literature / Fiction
El invierno en Lisboa / Antonio Muñoz Molina.	Literature / Fiction
La isla que se repite / Antonio Benítez Rojo.	Non Fiction

J

El jinete polaco / Antonio Muñoz Molina.	Literature / Fiction
Juan Bobo busca trabajo / Marisa Montes, and Joe Cepeda, il.	Children / Young Adults
Juan Pérez Jolote: biografía de un tzotzil / Ricardo Pozas.	Non Fiction
El juguete rabioso / Roberto Arlt.	Literature / Fiction
Julia / Georgina Lázaro, and Poli Marichal, il.	Children / Young Adults
Juvenilia / Miguel Cané.	Children / Young Adults
Juventud en éxtasis / Carlos Cuauhtémoc Sánchez.	Literature / Fiction

L

El laberinto de la soledad / Octavio Paz.	Non Fiction
El lápiz del carpintero / Manuel Rivas.	Literature / Fiction
El largo viaje / Jorge Semprún.	Non Fiction
Larra, anatomía de un dandy / Francisco Umbral.	Non Fiction
Latin American Studies: An Annotated Bibliography of Core Works / Ana María Cobos, and Ana Lya Sater.	Reference
Latinoamérica: su civilización y su cultura / Eugenio Chang-Rodriguez.	Non Fiction
Lautaro, joven libertador de Arauco / Fernando Alegría.	Children / Young Adults
El Lazarillo de Tormes / Anonymous.	Literature / Fiction
Le comieron la lengua los ratones / Silvia Molina, and Mari Rodríguez, il.	Children / Young Adults
El lector novohispano / José Joaquín Blanco, ed.	Literature / Fiction
Las lenguas de diamante / *Raíz salvaje* / Juana de Ibarbourou.	Poetry / Drama
Libro de buen amor / Juan Ruiz, Arcipreste de Hita.	Poetry / Drama

TITLES INDEX ●

Libro del Caballero Zifar / Anonymous.	Literature / Fiction
El libro del Conde Lucanor / Juan Manuel Infante de Castilla.	Literature / Fiction
El libro del frío / Antonio Gamoneda.	Poetry / Drama
Los libros arden mal / Manuel Rivas.	Literature / Fiction
Literatura centroamericana: diccionario de autores centroamericanos: fuentes para su estudio / Jorge Eduardo Arellano.	Reference
Literatura puertorriqueña: su proceso en el tiempo / Josefina Rivera de Álvarez.	Reference
Llámame Brooklyn / Eduardo Lago.	Literature / Fiction
Lo esencial en la ortografía / Francisco Alvero Francés.	Non Fiction
Lo fugitivo permanece. 20 cuentos mexicanos. / Carlos Monsiváis, ed.	Literature / Fiction
Lo que está en mi corazón / Marcela Serrano.	Literature / Fiction
Luces de bohemia / Ramón María del Valle-Inclán.	Poetry / Drama
La Llorona = The Weeping Woman: an Hispanic Legend Told in Spanish And English / Joe Hayes.	Children / Young Adults
La lluvia amarilla / Julio Llamazares.	Literature / Fiction

M

El mal mundo / Luis Antonio de Villena.	Literature / Fiction
Mala onda / Alberto Fuguet.	iterature / Fiction
Manual de traducción inglés/castellano / Gabriel López Guix, and J. Minnet Wilkinson.	Non Fiction
Manual del librero hispanoamericano / Antonio Palau y Dulcet.	Reference
Manuel Azaña: entre el mito y la leyenda / Ángeles Egido León.	Non Fiction
Mañanario / Ricardo Chávez Castañeda.	Children / Young Adults
Materia Prima: protonovela / Marcio Veloz Maggiolo.	Literature / Fiction

Melodrama / Jorge Franco.	Literature / Fiction
Memoria de la melancolía / María Teresa León.	Non Fiction
Memorias / Carlos Barral.	Non Fiction
Memorias / Josep Maria de Sagarra.	Non Fiction
Memorias de Altagracia / Salvador Garmendia.	Literature / Fiction
El mercado del libro antiguo español: una guía de precios / Julio Ollero, and Susana Bardón, eds.	Reference
Mi nombre es María Isabel / Alma Flor Ada.	Children / Young Adults
Miguel Vicente pata caliente / Orlando Araujo.	Children / Young Adults
Milagros de Nuestra Señora / Gonzalo de Berceo.	Literature / Fiction
Misión del bibliotecario y otros ensayos afines / José Ortega y Gasset.	Non Fiction
El misterio de la cripta embrujada / Eduardo Mendoza.	Literature / Fiction
Misteriosa Buenos Aires / Manuel Mújica Láinez.	Literature / Fiction
Mitología y artes prehispánicas de las Antillas / José Juan Arrom.	Non Fiction
La moneda de oro / Alma Flor Ada, and Neil Waldman, il.	Children / Young Adults
Morir en el intento / Jorge Ramos.	Non Fiction
La muerte de Artemio Cruz / Carlos Fuentes.	Literature / Fiction
La mujer del maestro / Guillermo Martínez.	Literature / Fiction
La mujer negra en la literatura puertorriqueña: cuentística de los setenta / Marie Ramos Rosado.	Non Fiction
Mujeres de ojos grandes / Ángeles Mastretta.	Literature / Fiction
Mujeres novelistas y novelas de mujeres en la posguerra española (1940-1965) / Raquel Conde Pen Alosa.	Reference
El mundo alucinante / Reinaldo Arenas.	Literature / Fiction

N

Nada / Carmen Laforet.	Literature / Fiction
Nadie encendía las lámparas y otros cuentos / Felisberto Hernández.	Literature / Fiction
Narraciones / Jorge Luis Borges.	Literature / Fiction
Naufragios y Comentarios / Alvar Núñez Cabeza de Vaca.	Non Fiction
Negrita / Onelio Jorge Cardoso.	Children / Young Adults
Niebla / Miguel de Unamuno.	Literature / Fiction
El niño que conversaba con la mar / Enrique Pérez Díaz.	Children / Young Adults
No amanece el cantor / José Ángel Valente.	Poetry / Drama
No será la tierra / Jorge Volpi.	Literature / Fiction
La noche de Tlatelolco / Elena Poniatowska.	Non Fiction
Noticias del extranjero / Pedro Lastra.	Poetry / Drama
Novelas ejemplares / Miguel de Cervantes.	Literature / Fiction
La novia de Odessa / Edgardo Cozarinsky.	Literature / Fiction
La novia oscura / Laura Restrepo.	Literature / Fiction
Nubosidad variable / Carmen Martín Gaite.	Literature / Fiction
Nueva enciclopedia de Puerto Rico / José A. Toro-Sugrañés.	Reference
Nueve novísimos poetas españoles / J.M. Castellet, selec.	Poetry / Drama

O

Obabakoak / Bernardo Atxaga.	Literature / Fiction
Obra poética / Jorge Luis Borges.	Poetry / Drama
Obra poética / Íñigo López de Mendoza Marqués de Santillana.	Poetry / Drama
Obra poética completa / Jorge Carrera Andrade.	Poetry / Drama

Obras completas (y otros cuentos) / Augusto Monterroso.	Literature / Fiction
Obras completas: poesía completa y prosa selecta / Alejandra Pizarnik.	Poetry / Drama
Obras escogidas / San Juan de la Cruz.	Poetry / Drama
El obsceno pájaro de la noche / José Donoso.	Literature / Fiction
Oficina N° 1 / Miguel Otero Silva.	Literature / Fiction
Ojo por diente / Rubén Bareiro Saguier.	Literature / Fiction
Los ojos de Judas y otros cuentos / Abraham Valdelomar.	Literature / Fiction
La ola latina: cómo los hispanos están transformando la política en los Estados Unidos / Jorge Ramos.	Non Fiction
Operación Hagen / Felipe Botaya.	Literature / Fiction
Oráculo manual y arte de prudencia / Baltasar Gracián.	Non Fiction
La orgía perpetua / Mario Vargas Llosa.	Non Fiction
Los orishas en Cuba / Natalia Bolívar Aróstegui.	Non Fiction
Ortografía de la lengua española. Edición revisada por las Academias de la Lengua Española / Real Academia Española.	Reference
Ortografía y ortotipografía del español actual / José Martínez de Sousa.	Reference
El oscurecer / Luis Mateo Díez.	Literature / Fiction
La otra mano de Lepanto / Carmen Boullosa.	Literature / Fiction

P

El país bajo mi piel / Gioconda Belli.	Non Fiction
El país de cuatro pisos y otros ensayos / José Luís González.	Non Fiction
Palabra sobre palabra: obra completa (1956-2001) / Ángel González.	Poetry / Drama
Una palabra tuya / Elvira Lindo.	Literature / Fiction

El palacio de la medianoche / Carlos Ruiz Zafón.	Children / Young Adults
Panorama de la prensa: temas contemporáneos del mundo hispano / Juan Kattan Ibarra.	Non Fiction
Pantaleón y las visitadoras / Mario Vargas Llosa.	Literature / Fiction
Paradiso / José Lezama Lima.	Literature / Fiction
Paraíso Travel / Jorge Franco.	Literature / Fiction
La parranda / Eduardo Blanco-Amor.	Literature / Fiction
Pasando página: autores y editores en la España democrática / Sergio Vila-Sanjuán.	Non Fiction
La pasión por los libros: un acercamiento a la bibliofilia / Francisco Mendoza Díaz-Maroto.	Non Fiction
Los pasos perdidos / Alejo Carpentier.	Literature / Fiction
Paula en Nueva York / Mikel Valverde.	Children / Young Adults
Los peces de la amargura / Fernando Aramburu.	Literature / Fiction
Pedrín y la garza / Hilda Perera, and Enrique Sánchez Moreiro, il.	Children / Young Adults
Pedro Páramo / Juan Rulfo.	Literature / Fiction
El peinado de la tía Chofi / Vivian Mansour Manzur, and Martha Avilés, il.	Children / Young Adults
La peineta colorada / Fernando Picó.	Children / Young Adults
Pequeñas resistencias: antología del nuevo cuento español / Andrés Neuman, ed.	Literature / Fiction
Percusión / José Balza.	Literature / Fiction
Perdido / Hilda Perera.	Children / Young Adults
Persona non grata / Jorge Edwards.	Non Fiction
Perspectivas culturales de Hispanoamérica / Juan Kattan Ibarra.	Non Fiction
El pez en en el agua: memorias / Mario Vargas Llosa.	Non Fiction
Pic-Nic. El triciclo. El laberinto / Fernando Arrabal.	Poetry / Drama

El príncipe moro / Fernando Paz Castillo.	Children / Young Adults
Prosas profanas / Rubén Darío.	Poetry / Drama
Puerto Rico la gran cocina del Caribe / José Díaz de Villegas.	Reference
Puerto Rico, cinco siglos de historia / Francisco Scarano.	Reference

QR

Los que falsificaron la firma de Dios / Viriato Sención.	Literature / Fiction
Rayuela / Julio Cortázar.	Literature / Fiction
La raza cómica: del sujeto en Puerto Rico / Rubén Ríos Ávila.	Non Fiction
La rebelión de las masas / José Ortega y Gasset.	Non Fiction
El recurso del Método / Alejo Carpentier.	Literature / Fiction
Redes: diccionario combinatorio del español contemporáneo / Ignacio de Bosque, dir.	Reference
La Regenta / Leopoldo Alas «Clarín».	Literature / Fiction
La reina del sur / Arturo Pérez-Reverte.	Literature / Fiction
El reino de este mundo / Alejo Carpentier.	Literature / Fiction
Relación acerca de las antigüedades de los indios / Fray Ramón Pané, and José Juan Arrom, ed.	Non Fiction
Renaissance and Baroque Poetry of Spain / Elias L. Rivers.	Poetry / Drama
Réquiem por un campesino español / Ramón J. Sender.	Literature / Fiction
Residuos de los tiempos / Enrique Laguerre.	Poetry / Drama
Respiración artificial / Ricardo Piglia.	Literature / Fiction
Respuesta a Sor Filotea / Sor Juana Inés de la Cruz.	Non Fiction
El retablo de las maravillas / Miguel de Cervantes.	Poetry / Drama
Reunión de cuentos / Jesús Gardea.	Literature / Fiction
Rimas / Gustavo Adolfo Bécquer.	Poetry / Drama

El río: novelas de caballería / Luis Cardoza y Aragón.	Non Fiction
Los ríos profundos / José María Arguedas.	Literature / Fiction
Los rojos de ultramar / Jordi Soler.	Literature / Fiction
Romancero Gitano / Federico García Lorca.	Poetry / Drama
La rosa intemporal / Rafael Heliodoro Valle.	Poetry / Drama
Rosario Tijeras / Jorge Franco.	Literature / Fiction
Rosas de papel / Olga Nolla.	Literature / Fiction
El rufián moldavo / Edgardo Cozarinsky.	Literature / Fiction
El rumor del tiempo / César Antonio Molina.	Poetry / Drama

S

San Manuel Bueno Mártir / Miguel de Unamuno.	Literature / Fiction
Semblanzas del corazón / José Rafael Lantigua.	Literature / Fiction
El señor Presidente / Miguel Ángel Asturias.	Literature / Fiction
Si te dicen que caí / Juan Marsé.	Literature / Fiction
El siglo de las luces / Alejo Carpentier.	Literature / Fiction
Sin noticias de Gurb / Eduardo Mendoza.	Literature / Fiction
Sin ti no soy yo / Lourdes Vázquez.	Literature / Fiction
Soldados / Francisco González Ledesma.	Literature / Fiction
Soldados de Salamina / Javier Cercas.	Literature / Fiction
Solitud / Víctor Català.	Literature / Fiction
Sólo cenizas hallarás (bolero) / Pedro Vergés.	Literature / Fiction
La sombra del viento / Carlos Ruiz Zafón.	Literature / Fiction
Son de Mar / Manuel Vicent.	Literature / Fiction
Sonetos / Luis de Góngora.	Poetry / Drama

Sóngoro cosongo / Nicolás Guillén.	Poetry / Drama
La sonrisa etrusca / José Luis Sampedro.	Literature / Fiction
Sopa de hortalizas = Vegetal soup / Ángeles Molina Iturrondo.	Children / Young Adults
Spiks / Pedro Juan Soto.	Literature / Fiction
Sueños y discursos / Francisco de Quevedo.	Literature / Fiction
El Sur; seguido de Bene / Adelaida García Morales.	Literature / Fiction

T

Tala / Gabriela Mistral.	Poetry / Drama
Teatro español de vanguardia / Agustín Muñoz-Alonso López, ed.	Poetry / Drama
Teatro español: (de la A a la Z) / Javier Huerta Calvo, Emilio Peral Vega, and Héctor Urzáiz Tortajada.	Reference
Tengo miedo torero / Pedro Lemebel.	Literature / Fiction
Teoría y práctica de la traducción / Valentín García Yebra.	Non Fiction
Terrazo / Abelardo Díaz Alfaro.	Literature / Fiction
Tesis de un homicidio / Diego Paszkowski.	Literature / Fiction
Tesoros de la poesía en la lengua castellana / Regino García-Badell.	Poetry / Drama
El testigo / Juan Villoro.	Literature / Fiction
La tierra de nadie / Alfonso Martínez-Mena.	Children / Young Adults
Tirant lo Blanc / Joanot Martorell.	Literature / Fiction
Traducción: literatura y literalidad / Octavio Paz.	Non Fiction
Traducción y traductología. Introducción a la traductología / Amparo Hurtado Albir.	Non Fiction
Tragicomedia mexicana: la vida en México de 1940 a 1970 / José Agustín.	Non Fiction
La travesía de Enrique / Sonia Nazario.	Non Fiction

U

V

La vida del Buscón / Francisco de Quevedo.	Literature / Fiction
La vida es sueño / Pedro Calderón de la Barca.	Poetry / Drama
La vida exagerada de Martín Romaña / Alfredo Bryce Echenique.	Literature / Fiction
Vida moderna hispana / James W. Brown.	Non Fiction
La vida perra de Juanita Narboni / Ángel Vázquez.	Literature / Fiction
El viento de la luna / Antonio Muñoz Molina.	Literature / Fiction
Vírgenes y mártires / Ana Lydia Vega.	Literature / Fiction
Visión de Anáhuac y otros ensayos / Alfonso Reyes.	Non Fiction
Vituperio (y algún elogio) de la errata / José Esteban.	Non Fiction
Vivir para contarla / Gabriel García Márquez.	Non Fiction
La vorágine / José Eustaquio Rivera.	Literature / Fiction
Vudú y magia en Santo Domingo / Carlos Esteban Deive.	Non Fiction
El vuelo de la reina / Tomás Eloy Martínez.	Literature / Fiction

YZ

Yo el supremo / Augusto Roa Bastos.	Literature / Fiction
Yo me perdono / Fietta Jarque.	Literature / Fiction
Los zapaticos de rosa / José Martí, and Lulu Delacre, il.	Children / Young Adults
El zoo de Pitus / Sebastià Sorribas.	Children / Young Adults
Zorro / Isabel Allende.	Literature / Fiction

TRANSLATED TITLES INDEX

A

An Account of the Antiquites of the Indians: Chronicles of the
New World Encounter / Fray Ramón Pané, and José Juan Arrom, ed.
(Spanish Title): *Relación acerca de las antigüedades de los indios* .... Non Fiction

The Adventures of the Ingenious Alfanhuí / Rafael Sánchez Ferlosio
(Spanish Title): *Industrias y andanzas de Alfanhuí* .... Literature / Fiction

El Aleph and Other Stories / Jorge Luis Borges
(Spanish Title): *El Aleph* .... Literature / Fiction

Altazor, or, a Voyage in a Parachute: Poem in VII Cantos / Vicente Huidobro
(Spanish Title): *Altazor o el viaje en paracaídas* .... Poetry / Drama

The Answer: Including a Selection of Poems / Sor Juana Inés de la Cruz
(Spanish Title): *Respuesta a Sor Filotea* .... Non Fiction

The Art of Worldly Wisdom: A Pocket Oracle / Baltasar Gracián
(Spanish Title): *Oráculo manual y arte de prudencia* .... Non Fiction

Artificial Respiration / Ricardo Piglia
(Spanish Title): *Respiración artificial* .... Literature / Fiction

Astonishing World: The Selected Poems of Ángel González, 1956-1986 /
Ángel González
(Spanish Title): *Palabra sobre palabra: obra completa (1956-2001)* .... Poetry / Drama

Ausiàs March: A Key Anthology / Ausiàs March
(Spanish Title): *Poesía* .... Poetry / Drama

The Autobiography of a Runaway Slave / Miguel Barnet
(Spanish Title): *Biografía de un cimarrón* .... Non Fiction

The Autobiography of Federico Sánchez and the Communist
Underground in Spain / Jorge Semprún
(Spanish Title): *Autobiografía de Federico Sánchez* .... Non Fiction

Averroes Middle Commentary on Porphyry's Isagoge / Averroes
(Spanish Title): *Comentario de la Isagogé de Porfirio* .... Non Fiction

B

The Back Room / Carmen Martín Gaite
(Spanish Title): *El cuarto de atrás* .... Literature / Fiction

Bad Vibes / Alberto Fuguet
(Spanish Title): *Mala onda* .... Literature / Fiction

Before Night Falls / Reinaldo Arenas
(Spanish Title): *Antes que anochezca: autobiografía* .... Literature / Fiction

Before We Were Free / Julia Álvarez
(Spanish Title): *Antes de ser libres* .... Children / Young Adults

Behind the Curtains / Carmen Martín Gaite
(Spanish Title): *Entre visillos* .... Literature / Fiction

Bless Me, Ultima / Rudolfo Anaya
(Spanish Title): *Última Bendíceme* .... Literature / Fiction

Blood Wedding / Federico García Lorca
(Spanish Title): *Bodas de sangre* .... Poetry / Drama

Bohemian Lights / Ramón María del Valle-Inclán
(Spanish Title): *Luces de bohemia* .... Poetry / Drama

Bomarzo / Manuel Mújica Láinez
(Spanish Title): *Bomarzo* .... Literature / Fiction

Book of Count Lucanor / Juan Manuel, Infante de Castilla
(Spanish Title): *El libro del Conde Lucanor* .... Literature / Fiction

The Book of Good Love / Juan Ruiz, Arcipreste de Hita
(Spanish Title): *Libro de buen amor* .... Poetry / Drama

Book of the Knight Zifar / Anonymous
(Spanish Title): *Libro del Caballero Zifar* .... Literature / Fiction

The Bride from Odessa / Edgardo Cozarinsky
(Spanish Title): *La novia de Odessa* .... Literature / Fiction

Burning Patience / Antonio Skármeta
(Spanish Title): *El cartero de Neruda: ardiente paciencia* .... Literature / Fiction

C

Canticles for Holy Mary / Alfonso X el Sabio
(Spanish Title): *Cantigas de Santa María* .... Poetry / Drama

Captain Pantoja and the Special Service / Mario Vargas Llosa
(Spanish Title): *Pantaleón y las visitadoras* .... Literature / Fiction

Caramelo / Sandra Cisneros
(Spanish Title): *Caramelo: puro cuento* .... Literature / Fiction

The Carpenter's Pencil / Manuel Rivas
(Spanish Title): *El lápiz del carpintero* .... Literature / Fiction

The Countryside of Níjar / Juan Goytisolo
(Spanish Title): *Campos de Níjar* .... Non Fiction

The Criterion / Jaume Balmes
(Spanish Title): *El Criterio* .... Non Fiction
Cronopios and Famas / Julio Cortázar
(Spanish Title): *Historias de cronopios y de famas* .... Literature / Fiction

Crossing Over: A Mexican Family on the Migrant Trail / Rubén Martínez
(Spanish Title): *Cruzando la frontera: la crónica implacable de una
familia mexicana que emigra a Estados Unidos* .... Non Fiction

The Cypresses Believe in God / José María Gironella
(Spanish Title): *Los cipreses creen en Dios* .... Literature / Fiction

D

The Dark Bride / Laura Restrepo
(Spanish Title): *La novia oscura* .... Literature / Fiction

The Death of Artemio Cruz / Carlos Fuentes
(Spanish Title): *La muerte de Artemio Cruz* .... Literature / Fiction

Deep Rivers / José María Arguedas
(Spanish Title): *Los ríos profundos* .... Literature / Fiction

Delirium / Laura Restrepo
(Spanish Title): *Delirio* .... Literature / Fiction

A Dictionary of Symbols / Juan Eduardo Cirlot
(Spanish Title): *Diccionario de símbolos* .... Reference

Dirty Havana Trilogy / Pedro Juan Gutiérrez
(Spanish Title): *Trilogía sucia de La Habana* .... Literature / Fiction

Don Quixote / Miguel de Cervantes
(Spanish Title): *Don Quijote de la Mancha* .... Literature / Fiction

Dostoevsky's Last Night / Cristina Peri Rossi
(Spanish Title): *La última noche de Dostoievski* .... Literature / Fiction

Dreams and Discourses / Francisco de Quevedo
(Spanish Title): *Sueños y discursos* .... Literature / Fiction

Dying to Cross / Jorge Ramos
(Spanish Title): *Morir en el intento* .... Non Fiction

E

Encyclopedia Latina: History, Culture and Society in the United States /
Stavans, Ilan, ed., and Harold Augenbraum, assoc. ed.
(In English) ....Reference

Encyclopedia of Contemporary Latin American and Caribbean Cultures /
Balderston, Daniel, Mike Gonzalez, and Ana M. López, eds.
(In English) ....Reference

Encyclopedia of Contemporary Spanish Culture / Rodgers, Eamonn, ed.
(In English) ....Reference

Encyclopedia of Latin American History and Culture /
Tenembaum, Barbara A., and Georgette M. Dorn, eds.
(In English) ....Reference

Enrique's Journey / Sonia Nazario
(Spanish Title): *La travesía de Enrique* .... Non Fiction

Eva Luna / Isabel Allende
(Spanish Title): *Eva Luna* ....Literature / Fiction

Exemplary Stories / Miguel de Cervantes
(Spanish Title): *Novelas ejemplares* ....Literature / Fiction

F

The Fallen / Juan Marsé
(Spanish Title): *Si te dicen que caí* ....Literature / Fiction

The Family of Pacual Duarte / Camilo José Cela
(Spanish Title): *La familia de Pascual Duarte* ....Literature / Fiction

Farabeuf / Salvador Elizondo
(Spanish Title): *Farabeuf* ....Literature / Fiction

The Feast of the Goat / Mario Vargas Llosa
(Spanish Title): *La fiesta del Chivo* ....Literature / Fiction

Federico García Lorca / Ian Gibson
(Spanish Title): *Federico García Lorca* .... Non Fiction

The Firefly Spanish/English Visual Dictionary /
Jean-Claude Corbeil, and Ariane Archambault ....Reference

A Fish in the Water: a Memoir / Mario Vargas Llosa
(Spanish Title): *El pez en en el agua: memorias* .... Non Fiction

G

H

I

JK

The Kingdom of this World / Alejo Carpentier
(Spanish Title): El reino de este mundo .... Literature / Fiction

Kiss of the Spider Woman / Manuel Puig
(Spanish Title): El beso de la mujer araña .... Literature / Fiction

L

The Labyrinth of Solitude, the Other Mexico, and Other Essays / Octavio Paz
(Spanish Title): El laberinto de la soledad .... Non Fiction

The Landscape of Castile / Antonio Machado
(Spanish Title): Campos de Castilla .... Poetry / Drama

The Last Cato: A Novel / Matilde Asensi
(Spanish Title): El último Catón .... Literature / Fiction

The Latin Wave: How Hispanics are Transforming Politics in the United States /
Jorge Ramos
(Spanish Title): La ola latina: cómo los hispanos están
transformando la política en los Estados Unidos .... Non Fiction

Lautaro / Fernando Alegría
(Spanish Title): Lautaro, joven libertador de Arauco .... Children / Young Adults

A Library for Juana: The World of Sor Juana Inés / Pat Mora
(Spanish Title): Una biblioteca para Juana: el mundo de Sor Juana Inés ...... Children / Young Adults

Life is a Dream / Pedro Calderón de la Barca
(Spanish Title): La vida es sueño .... Poetry / Drama

The Life of a Swindler / Francisco de Quevedo
(Spanish Title): La vida del Buscón .... Literature / Fiction

The Life of Lazarillo de Tormes / Anonymous
(Spanish Title): El Lazarillo de Tormes .... Literature / Fiction

Like Water for Chocolate: A Novel in Monthly Installments, with
Recipes, Romances, and Home Remedies / Laura Esquivel
(Spanish Title): Como agua para chocolate .... Literature / Fiction

Living to Tell the Tale / Gabriel García Márquez
(Spanish Title): Vivir para contarla .... Non Fiction

La Llorona = The Weeping Woman: An Hispanic Legend Told in Spanish
and English / Joe Hayes .... Children / Young Adults

The Long Voyage / Jorge Semprún
(Spanish Title): El largo viaje .... Non Fiction

The Lost Steps / Alejo Carpentier
(Spanish Title): Los pasos perdidos .... Literature / Fiction

Love in the Time of Cholera / Gabriel García Márquez
(Spanish Title): El amor en los tiempos de cólera .... Literature / Fiction

Lyrical Poems / Lope de Vega
(Spanish Title): Poesías líricas .... Poetry / Drama

M

Macho Camacho's Beat / Luis Rafael Sánchez
(Spanish Title): La guaracha del Macho Camacho .... Literature / Fiction

Mad Toy / Roberto Arlt
(Spanish Title): El juguete rabioso .... Literature / Fiction

The Magic Theatre / Miguel de Cervantes
(Spanish Title): El retablo de las maravillas .... Poetry / Drama

The Maravillas District / Rosa Chacel
(Spanish Title): Barrio de maravillas .... Literature / Fiction

Massacre in Mexico / Elena Poniatowska
(Spanish Title): La noche de Tlatelolco .... Non Fiction

Memories of Altagracia / Salvador Garmendia
(Spanish Title): Memorias de Altagracia .... Literature / Fiction

Mexican Bolero / Ángeles Mastretta
(Spanish Title): Arráncame la vida .... Literature / Fiction

Miracles of Our Lady / Gonzalo de Berceo
(Spanish Title): Milagros de Nuestra Señora .... Literature / Fiction

The Mission of the Librarian / José Ortega y Gasset
(Spanish Title): Misión del bibliotecario y otros ensayos afines .... Non Fiction

Mist: A Tragicomic Novel / Miguel de Unamuno
(Spanish Title): Niebla .... Literature / Fiction

N

O

P

QR

S

The Savage Detectives / Roberto Bolaño
(Spanish Title): *Los detectives salvajes* ....Literature / Fiction

Selected Poems / Gabriela Mistral
(Spanish Title): *Tala* .... Poetry / Drama

The Selected Poems of Miguel Hernández / Miguel Hernández
(Spanish Title): *Cancionero y romancero de ausencias* .... Poetry / Drama

Selected Poetry / Francisco de Quevedo
(Spanish Title): *Poesía varia* .... Poetry / Drama

Selected Verses / Federico García Lorca
(Spanish Title): *Antología poética* .... Poetry / Drama

Selected Works / San Juan de la Cruz
(Spanish Title): *Obras escogidas* .... Poetry / Drama

Selected Writings / Rubén Darío
(Spanish Title): *Prosas profanas* .... Poetry / Drama

The Shadow of the Wind / Carlos Ruiz Zafón
(Spanish Title): *La sombra del viento*.....................................Literature / Fiction

Short Stories / María Elena Walsh
(Spanish Title): *Pocopán* .... Children / Young Adults

Shorts: Stories / Alberto Fuguet
(Spanish Title): *Cortos* ....Literature / Fiction

The Shrouded Woman / María Luisa Bombal
(Spanish Title): *La amortajada* ....Literature / Fiction

Soldiers of Salamis / Javier Cercas
(Spanish Title): *Soldados de Salamina* ....Literature / Fiction

Solitude: A Novel / Víctor Català
(Spanish Title): *Solitud* ....Literature / Fiction

Songs of Life and Hope / Rubén Darío
(Spanish Title): *Azul. Cantos de Vida y Esperanza* .... Poetry / Drama

Sonnets / Luis de Góngora
(Spanish Title): *Sonetos* .... Poetry / Drama

The South; and, Bene / Adelaida García Morales
(Spanish Title): *El Sur; seguido de Bene* ....Literature / Fiction

The Spaniards: An Introduction to their History / Américo Castro
(Spanish Title): *España en su historia* .... Non Fiction

Spiks: Stories / Pedro Juan Soto
(Spanish Title): *Spiks* .... Literature / Fiction

Stories and Poems / Rubén Darío
(Spanish Title): *Azul* .... Poetry / Drama

The Story of a Seagull and the Cat Who Taught Her to Fly / Luis Sepúlveda
(Spanish Title): *Historia de una gaviota y del gato que le enseñó a volar* .... Literature / Fiction

The Storyteller / Mario Vargas Llosa
(Spanish Title): *El hablador* .... Literature / Fiction

The Suspect Truth / Juan Ruiz de Alarcón
(Spanish Title): *La verdad sospechosa* .... Literature / Fiction

T

Tales Our Abuelitas Told: A Hispanic Folktale Collection /
F. Isabel Campoy, and Alma Flor Ada
(Spanish Title): *Cuentos que contaban nuestras abuelas* .... Children / Young Adults

Tarzan's Tonsillitis / Alfredo Bryce Echenique
(Spanish Title): *La amigdalitis de Tarzán* .... Literature / Fiction

They Forged the Signature of God / Viriato Sención
(Spanish Title): *Los que falsificaron la firma de Dios* .... Literature / Fiction

Thine is the Kingdom / Abilio Estévez
(Spanish Title): *Tuyo es el reino* .... Literature / Fiction

Three Trapped Tigers / Guillermo Cabrera Infante
(Spanish Title): *Tres tristes tigres* .... Literature / Fiction

The Time of the Doves / Mercè Rodoreda
(Spanish Title): *La plaza del diamante* .... Literature / Fiction

Tirant lo Blanc / Joanot Martorell
(Spanish Title): *Tirant lo Blanc* .... Literature / Fiction

The Tragic Sense of Life in Men and Nations / Miguel de Unamuno
(Spanish Title): *Del sentimiento trágico de la vida* .... Non Fiction

The Tree of Knowledge / Pío Baroja
(Spanish Title): *El árbol de la ciencia* .... Literature / Fiction

The Trickster of Seville / Tirso de Molina
(Spanish Title): *El burlador de Sevilla* .... Poetry / Drama

COLLABORATORS INDEX

A-Z

Sabrina Abreu, Instituto Cervantes New York Library

Lluís Agustí, Instituto Cervantes New York Library

Ismael Alicea, The New York Public Library

Sarah Aponte, Dominican Studies Institute, CUNY, Librarian

Daniel Berdaner, Dallas Public Library

Martha Berman, Professor of Language and Literature

Florencio Bernal, Reader

David Block, Cornell University Library

Santiago Cabanas, Consul General of Spain in Miami

F. Isabel Campoy, Transformative Education

Pedro Canó, Instituto Cervantes New York, Professor

Ramón Caraballo, Librería Barco de Papel, Bookseller

Paloma Celis Carbajal, UW-Madison Library

Teresa Chapa, University of North Carolina at Chapel Hill

José María Conget, Writer

Yara Larie Cruz, Universal Career Community College, Librarian

Patricia Cuesta, Los Angeles Public Library

Juan Pablo Debesis, Lectorum, Bookseller

Bernat Dedéu, Cadena Ser, Correspondent

María José Durán Silva, G.W.: Carver Middle School

Angela Encinas, San Bernardino Public Library

Patricia Figueroa, Brown University Library, Iberian and Latin American Studies Librarian

Mónica Flores-Correa, Professor and Writer

Xosé Luis García Canido, Instituto Cervantes, Cultural Director

Silvia Gil de Cwilich, Artist and Reader

Adan Griego, Stanford University Libraries

Diego Hernández, Colegio Doral Academy Middle School

Bruno Hernández Piché, Mexican Writer and Diplomat

Richard Heyer, Instituto Cervantes New York Library

Angélica Hurtado-Gracia, Los Angeles Public Library

Eduardo Lago, Instituto Cervantes New York, Director

Eduardo Lamadrid, Trans-Lingual Communications Inc., Translator, Writer and Editor

Jeffry Larson, Yale University Library

Tom LaSalle, Ferguson Library

Georgina Lazaro, Writer

Isaías Lerner, The City University of New York CUNY

Elvira Lindo, Writer and Journalist

Alfons Luna, AFP New York, Journalist

Nashieli Marcano, University of Akron, Assistant Professor of Bibliography Science and Technology Librarian

Jaume Martí Olivella, University of New Hampshire

Marko Miletich, Binghamton University (SUNY)

Teresa Mlawer, Lectorum Publications Inc., Editor

Gaspar Orozco, Mexican Poet and Diplomat

Gabriel Partlow, Pima County Public Library

Mark Pendleton, Branigan Library Las Cruces NM

Ernesto Pérez Zúñiga, Instituto Cervantes, Director of Cultural Activities

Christine Peterson, Maranatha Academy

Claude Potts, Arizona State University, Latin American & Iberian Studies Librarian

Guillermina Raffo Magnasco, St Thomas University

Blanca Riestra, Instituto Cervantes Albuquerque, Director

Julio Rivas, Reader

Miriam Rodriguez, Dallas Public Library

Libbhy Romero, Brooklyn Public Library

Alina San Juan, Trade Comission of Spain

Alvaro Sanabria, San Francisco Public Library

Ángel Santiago Cervantes, Cahesa

Lynn Shirey, Harvard College Library

Millie Torrance, Sacramento Public Library

Miguel Valladares, Dartmouth College, Librarian

Scott Van Jacob, University of Notre Dame, Librarian

Fernando Velázquez Medina, Writer and Journalist

Salvador Vergara, Instituto Cervantes Chicago Library

Juan Carlos Vidal, Instituto Cervantes Chicago, Director

Carmen de Zulueta, Writter and Professor

GENERAL INDEX